FORGED BY FIRE

Maryland's National Guard at the Great Baltimore Fire of 1904

Dean K. Yates

WITH FOREWORD BY
Harold A. Williams

HERITAGE BOOKS
2011

HERITAGE BOOKS
AN IMPRINT OF HERITAGE BOOKS, INC.

Books, CDs, and more—Worldwide

For our listing of thousands of titles see our website
at
www.HeritageBooks.com

Published 2011 by
HERITAGE BOOKS, INC.
Publishing Division
100 Railroad Ave. #104
Westminster, Maryland 21157

Copyright © 1992 Dean K. Yates

Cover photo: Guardsmen posted on East Baltimore Street warm themselves near a small fire. The sixteen-story burned hulk of the Continental Trust Building, situated at the corner of Calvert and East Baltimore Streets, looms in the background. (Peale Museum, Baltimore City Life Museums)

Library of Congress Cataloging in Publication Data

Yates, Dean K., 1953-

Forged by Fire: Maryland's National Guard at the Great Baltimore Fire of 1904

1. Baltimore (Md.)-History-20th century. 2. Armed forces-mobilization.
3. Guards troops-Maryland. 4. Fires-Maryland. 5. Disasters-Maryland.

Library of Congress Catalog Card Number: 92-74411

Book design and composition by Maryland State Archives

Edward C. Papenfuse, State Archivist
Lynne Browne, Director, Computer Services
David Williams, Composition Specialist

All rights reserved. No part of this book may be reproduced or transmitted in any form or by any means, electronic or mechanical, including photocopying, recording or by any information storage and retrieval system without written permission from the author, except for the inclusion of brief quotations in a review.

International Standard Book Numbers
Paperbound: 978-0-940907-22-5
Clothbound: 978-0-7884-8613-5

For the present and former doctors, nurses, and staff of wards 71 and 78 at Walter Reed Army Medical Center, Washington, DC, especially Doctor Jeffrey K. Giguere, Carolyn Bailey, and Jackie Lownie who provided me with a second chance at life. And the present and former staff members of the Veterans Administration's Vocational Rehabilitation Office in Baltimore, MD, especially Len Addington, Connie Bauer, Andy Dombrowski, and Dalphine Kinch, who provided me with a second chance at a career.

Contents

Preface	vii
Part One: The Guard's service at the Great Fire	1
Notes	23
Abbreviations	31
Part Two: Roster of Guardsmen Who Served at the Great Fire	33
Bibliography	94
Index	97

Illustrations

Maps and Charts

1. Map illustrating burned district   1

2. Chart indicating daily high and low temperatures as well as wind chill range   9

Photographs

1. Baltimore's central business district before the fire   viii

2. Same area of the city after the fire   viii

3. First Regiment mess tent   7

4. Navy and Army guardsmen   8

5. Three guardsmen pose in burned district   10

6. Soldiers' shelter   11

7. Labor Lyceum   13

8. Perimeter duty on East Lexington Street   15

9. Guardsmen marching on East Baltimore Street   18

10. Officer on horseback addresses sentry   19

Foreword

Dean K. Yates's account of the Maryland National Guard's service during and immediately following the Great Baltimore Fire of 1904 is an important and fascinating addition to the history of that catastrophe. Importantly too, this history describes the precedent setting role that the Fire had in shaping the turn-of-the-century Guard. The Guard's activation during the Great Baltimore Fire represents its first response to a civil disaster.

This history was written originally as a graduate project while Yates was a student at the University of Maryland Baltimore County. Based upon documents from the Adjutant General's files in the Maryland State Archives, this is the first full and significant telling of the Guard's role in the two-day fire and its aftermath.

More than 2,000 guardsmen were called up, not only from Baltimore, but from across Maryland, and then remained on duty for 17 days. Under the command of the First Brigade, units on duty included the First, Fourth, and Fifth regiments; Signal Corps; Troop A Calvary; and Naval Brigade. Though untrained in crowd control, they performed wide-ranging duties, including ejecting intoxicated men from the bar of a burning hotel.

The book's energetic account sparkles with anecdote and telling detail. For example: Mayor Robert McLane climbing into the City Hall belfry to sound the riot call, "three-three's rung about six times" ... Guardsmen breaking into an armory from the roof of an adjoining building ... Frantic civilians using fraudulent passes in attempts to gain entrance to the burned district ... Calvarymen dining at the exclusive Atheneum Club.

My history of the Fire, *Baltimore Afire*, first published in 1954 on the fiftieth anniversary of the Fire, contains a limited account of the Maryland National Guard's role in addition to a few pictures of the guardsmen. I wish I had the ingenuity Dean K. Yates used in searching out the Guard's role. It would have enhanced my history.

Harold A. Williams

Preface

I discovered the core materials on which this book is based in August 1991 while working at the Maryland State Archives as project archivist for a National Historical Publications and Records Commission (NHPRC) project. The federally funded project is designed to describe all state documents presently held by the Archives, which date to 1634. Through the efforts of such descriptive undertakings, archives across the nation are promoting better access to their holdings, thus encouraging greater use by researchers. Like many documents in repositories everywhere, the national guard rosters and officer reports had lain for decades, unused.

The work which culminated in this book began as a final paper to fulfill the requirements of a Masters of Arts degree in history at the University of Maryland Baltimore County (UMBC). Professor Joseph L. Arnold of UMBC directed my research and writing efforts and professor Colin B. Burke helped me establish parameters for a statistical evaluation of information gleaned from the payrolls.

Professor Arnold, Madeleine Hughes, Doug McElrath, and Julie Whitcomb read various drafts of the manuscript an recommended some thoughtful changes. Several colleagues at the Maryland State Archives also supported my work and contributed to this publication. Among them are Lynne Browne, Teresa Fountain, Jim Hefelfinger, Tim Pyatt, Mame Warren, and Dave Williams. State Archivist Edward C. Papenfuse also helped and encouraged my efforts. I am especially indebted to Gregory A. Stiverson, assistant state archivist, for his unfailing support of this project.

Additional support was provided by local repositories and agencies. I would like to thank Rebecca Gunby and Tom Cotter of the Baltimore City Archives, Mary Markey of the Peale Museum, and Mike Musick of the National Archives. Furthermore, Colonel Ernest M. Snyder of the Maryland National Guard opened the Fifth Regiment's archives for my study, Mr. Ken Shaver of the Baltimore Weather Service at the Baltimore-Washington International Airport granted me access to 1904 weather data, Schneidereith & Sons allowed me to reprint the map of the burned district, and officer Len Petrovich of the Baltimore City Police Department twice assisted my search for pertinent arrest records.

I saved my heaviest debts for last. Jenny and Nichelle managed to survive the last few years, when dad was more often working, studying, or in school than at home. And finally, to my wife, Kathy, thank you for the past five years. Now it's your turn to go to school.

The Guard's Service at the Great Fire

Baltimore burned from February seventh to eighth, 1904. Newspaper "Extras," which appeared within hours of the fire's outbreak, described it in apocalyptic imagery, such as "Deluge of Seething Flame." The destructive force of the fire inevitably led some to compare it with the Chicago Fire of 1871.

Once the fire was contained, messages of sympathy and stories of heroic firemen replaced the initial, too-often sensational reports. Baltimoreans turned their attention to the job of rebuilding that lay ahead. Eighty-six blocks of Baltimore's central business district, consisting of more than 2,400 businesses, lay in ruins. Despite the devastation, however, the city was rebuilt within a few years and the catastrophe faded into history. [1]

Although Baltimore's Great Fire of 1904 is one of those landmark events in the state's history that is familiar to most Marylanders, many are unaware of the essential service provided by the Maryland National Guard in the conflagration's aftermath. From the seventh to the twenty-third of February, over 2,000 Maryland guardsmen patrolled the burned district, faced an often obstinate citizenry, and endured extreme hardship. Their actions were unprecedented in Maryland. While today national guardsmen are usually activated during times of flood, hurricane, tornado, or other natural or manmade disasters, in Maryland that tradition began with the Guard's response to the Great Baltimore Fire in 1904. This is their story.

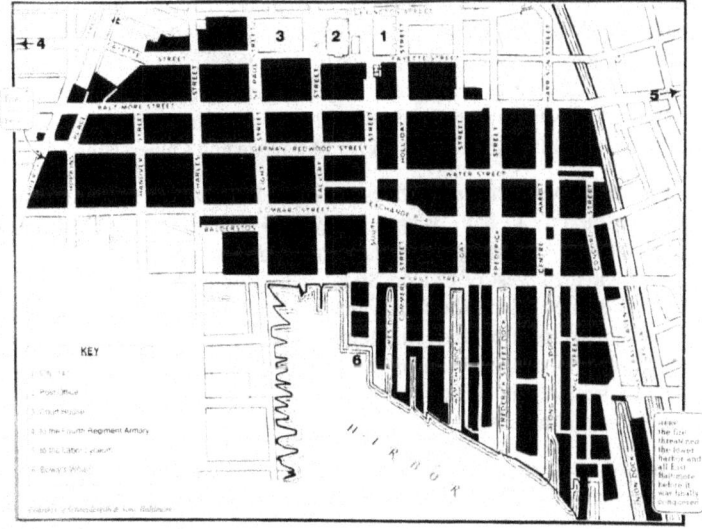

Map of burned district

"Desperate fire here. Must have help at once."

At 10:48 A.M. on Sunday, February 7, 1904, a heat-sensitive alarm in the basement of the John E. Hurst Building, located on the southeast corner of Liberty and German streets, sounded the first warning. Within a few minutes, an explosion rocked the structure, spreading firebrands to adjacent buildings. It did not take long for Baltimore's Fire Chief, George W. Horton, to recognize an impending danger. Before noon he appealed to Washington, D.C. fire officials for help. [2]

Throughout the day, the fire raced northeastward, driven by intensifying winds. In the fire's wake, Baltimore's central business district was chaotic. Huge crowds watched the fire, which raged uncontrolled despite the best efforts of the city's large and efficient fire department. Businessmen added to the pandemonium by hiring every available wagon and dray in a frantic attempt to salvage what they could from doomed offices. Desperate city officials, hoping to establish a fire break, ordered some buildings dynamited. Demolition had the opposite effect, however, sparking new fires. As nightfall approached, unable to establish order or control the fire, Baltimore leaders turned their attention to securing the city.[3]

At 5:30 P.M., Brigadier General Lawrason Riggs, Commander of the Maryland National Guard's First Brigade, met with George M. Upshur, President of Baltimore's Board of Police Commissioners in the City Hall. Citing the provisions of Article 34 of the State Militia Law, Upshur ordered out the Fourth and Fifth regiments to encircle the fire area. Their mission, he announced, was to "exclude the public...and [prevent] looting." Two hours after his meeting with Upshur, Riggs ordered the regimental commanders to assemble their units. He further ordered that as company-sized units of twenty men were outfitted, they were to report to him at Brigade Headquarters in City Hall, located at the corner of Fayette and Calvert streets.[4]

While he waited for units to report, Riggs formulated a plan of action. He divided the city in half, using his City Hall headquarters as the northernmost border. According to the plan, units from the Fourth Regiment would secure the area west of Calvert Street to prevent crowds from entering the burned district behind the fire, which was still advancing to the northeast. Meanwhile, units from the Fifth Regiment were to be dispatched east of Calvert Street to march ahead of the flames, clearing that area of civilians. Riggs's simple plan constituted the basis for all National Guard tactics until the fire was extinguished.

In the meantime, regimental commanders discovered that their units were not prepared to be called out on such short notice. Most officers and men were among the crowd watching the fire, so attempts to notify them by telephone and telegram proved ineffective. Beginning just after 7:30, commanders dispatched officers and men who ran through the neighborhoods searching out other guardsmen and spreading word of the call-up. The riot call, consisting of three series of three bells, was finally sounded at 9 P.M. on the City Hall bell. Upon hearing it, hundreds of guardsmen reported for duty. Established to muster the militia in just such an emergency, Riggs and Upshur apparently forgot about the alarm, or perhaps in the new era of telephonic communication, simply failed to recognize the benefit of using the outmoded system.[5]

Reporting for duty, guardsmen encountered obstacles that delayed deployment. A compartmentalized storage arrangement within their armories meant that uniforms were locked in company rooms while rifles and other necessary equipment were secured in separate storerooms. Only company commanders, ordnance officers, and regimental quartermasters, respectively, had keys to the lockers. Those who reported early, therefore, found essential equipment locked beyond their reach.

When Colonel Henry M. Warfield, Fifth Regiment Commander, arrived at the North Howard Street armory at about 8 P.M., he found two officers and several enlisted men waiting for someone to open the building. Warfield unlocked the armory and designated Lieutenant W. Pinkney Holmes as "acting quartermaster." Not having a key, Holmes broke into the quartermaster's storeroom and began to issue equipment. As his men were equipped, Warfield ordered them into the city to "bring in" any regimental members they could find.[6]

Members of the Fourth Regiment also found themselves locked out at their armory on West Fayette Street. At twenty minutes past eight, unable to reach the Regiment Commander, Lieutenant Colonel J. Frank Supplee assumed command. On his orders, two men broke into the armory from the roof of an adjoining building while Supplee and others "forced the outside gates." Once inside, locks on quartermaster and company storerooms were forced. Whereas an acting quartermaster issued equipment at the Fifth Regiment armory, members of the Fourth Regiment helped themselves to needed supplies.[7]

By 9 P.M., having overcome such obstacles, the first company left the Fourth Regiment armory. Under command of Captain Bruce B. Gootee, the unit consisted of two sergeants, three corporals, and eight privates. When Gootee arrived at Brigade Headquarters at about 9:30, Riggs directed him to report to Police Marshal Thomas F. Farnan at South and Baltimore streets "with orders to keep the crowd back as the fire approached and to use [his] own judgement." As subsequent units from the Fourth reported to him, Riggs positioned them to the west and southwest, encircling the west boundary of the burned district. By midnight, the Fourth Regiment's line extended to the corner of Pratt and Howard streets.[8]

Large crowds of curious men, women, and children tested the Fourth Regiment's picket line. Untrained in crowd control tactics, some units responded with force when pressed by spectators. Lieutenant Colonel Supplee, for example, reported that he was "frequently compelled to draw [his] sword" to assist his men by "forcing the crowd back with the flat of the blade." A similar show of force was used by Lieutenant J. E. Rittenhouse when he deployed his men with rifles held at port arms and bayonets fixed. Rittenhouse's actions drove the crowd more than a block, from just south of Lexington Street northward across Saratoga, which formed the northern perimeter maintained by the Fourth Regiment.[9]

Even though Saratoga Street was two blocks north of the burned district, Major Harry C. Jones reported that it was the "scene of the wildest confusion." "Utmost vigilance," he continued, "was required to prevent loot[ers], Carriages, Wagons and conveyances of every description" from breaching the sentry line. In one incident, according to Jones's report, a horse was "severely injured by a sentry's bayonet" when its teamster attempted to force his way past the guards at the corner of Saratoga and Howard streets. While most officers from the Fourth reported large and sometimes determined crowds, Jones was the only one to report such belligerence.[10]

As units of the Fourth secured the fire's rear flank, elements of the Fifth moved ahead of the flames. At 9:30 P.M. Captain Washington Bowie, Jr. commanded the first company to leave the Fifth Regiment armory. His thirty-man provisional company consisted of three men from Company G, two men from Company H, four men from Company L, and twenty-one men from Company F, his regular unit. When they arrived at Brigade Headquarters twenty minutes later, Bowie was directed to South and Water streets with orders to clear the area and retreat eastward as the fire approached. At that time Bowie's was the only unit available to clear an approximately twelve block area from Light Street to the Jones Falls between Water and Pratt streets. In addition, they were directed to evacuate the wharves and other areas along the waterfront.

In the process of clearing the area, one of Bowie's junior officers reported that his men encountered "numbers" of intoxicated men who had congregated in saloons. Company F Executive Officer, First Lieutenant S. E. Conradt, recounted the situation in greater detail. He reported having to break into a burning hotel at the corner of Pratt and West Falls streets to eject about a dozen men. Conradt reasoned that the patrons, "attracted by the fine liquor[,]...were saving it in the most approved fashion." In addition to the twelve at the bar, guardsmen discovered another man on the building's roof, holding "a single bucket of water"! When he refused to leave, guardsmen carried him from the hotel. "This building," Conradt added, "burned to the ground within thirty minutes."[11]

After midnight, as flames raced eastward, fire officials from the city and surrounding municipalities decided to take a stand at the Jones Falls. This was a natural fire break that they believed would provide the best opportunity to contain the blaze. The firemen's strategy also furnished General Riggs with the first occasion to coordinate Guard tactics with civilian efforts to extinguish the fire.

At 1 A.M., Riggs ordered Major John Hinkley to lead a battalion to the east side of the fire, "driving back the crowds, and making room for the [fire] engines." Fifteen minutes later, Hinkley assembled provisional companies A, B, E, and L in the Court House square on Calvert Street. Hinkley marched the battalion east on Fayette Street and then south to the area of the Jones Falls, posting companies at Frederick and Water streets, Fayette and Harrison streets, and Baltimore and Front streets. The last post, reported Hinkley, was already held by a Fourth Regiment company commanded by "Capt. Bokee." At 2:15 A.M., Hinkley established the Fifth Regimental headquarters on the corner of Baltimore and Front streets in Sherman's Drugstore and then marched his remaining men westward toward the Jones Falls and the approaching fire. [12]

As Company F had done in the area farther west, Hinkley's battalion worked quickly to clear hotels and saloons of drunken men, at least one of whom had to be carried by guardsmen across a bridge over the Jones Falls. In another case, after the door of a saloon on Albemarle Street was shut in his face and locked, Hinkley ordered it broken down and then ejected all the bar's occupants. Once the western side of the Jones Falls was evacuated, Hinkley's battalion pushed back the spectators, sometimes as far eastward as High Street, to allow firemen and their equipment enough room in which to work. The crowds, Hinkley reported, were "very orderly...[and] readily submissive to orders with reasonable courtesy." Unlike the show of force made by some elements of the Fourth Regiment, Hinkley asserted that "in forcing back the crowds I kept bayonets unfixed."[13]

Colonel Warfield, Hinkley's regimental commander, also reported on the Fifth's evacuation activity in the vicinity of the Jones Falls. Unlike his line officers' reports, however, Warfield's account exhibited a stereotypical view of the residents in that area of Baltimore. "The Center Market Space," wrote the colonel, "was thickly populated by the more ignorant classes." Accordingly, he praised his units for "driving these people East of the Falls."[14]

Newspaper accounts of the evacuation provide an additional interpretation. Like Warfield's report, one paper's point of view was founded on social bias. "Even in their daily routine of life," it reported, "the foreign element who lived [in the area] were hysterical." According to the article, on the night of the fire guardsmen were confronted by crowds of men, women, and "numerous children" who refused to leave their houses. At one point, the paper announced, guardsmen had "literally [to] drag a woman from her bed."

Yet another perspective was provided by Baltimore's *Afro-American Ledger*. In one article the paper declared that the activity within the "Eastern Section [was] so wild as to beggar description," but another article focused on the fire zone's common denominator: the "provident and improvident alike suffered...in the frantic excitement there was no class or creed."[15]

After all persons were evacuated to East Baltimore, guardsmen were reassigned to their normal units. At about that time, Colonel Warfield reassigned Hinkley's battalion from crowd control to fire fighting. Responsible for the area south of Lombard Street to the harbor, the performance of Hinkley's battalion was critical. It was not yet dawn when wind-driven flames approached the battalion's position from the northwest. Up to that time firemen had prevented the fire from leaping the Jones Falls, but the presence of several lumber companies and woodworking manufacturers on the lower end of East Falls Avenue jeopardized their strategy. Millions of board feet of lumber lay exposed to firebrands blown on 30 mph winds.

Hinkley and his officers detailed guardsmen to extinguish incipient fires that broke out in the lumber yards. At one point the major ordered a "small pile of lumber" thrown into the falls. Battalion members were also called upon to clear the crowds from the President Street Railway Station to allow railroad employees the opportunity to protect their property in case the fire crossed the Jones Falls. The officer in charge of that action reported that as the fire approached his men were "obliged to leave [the area] on account of the heat." The President Street Station, however, did not burn and the Jones Falls line held.[16]

By dawn on the fire's second day, strong northwest winds turned the path of the flames toward the harbor. With the threat of fire spreading to East Baltimore thereby greatly diminished, Hinkley was able to relieve his companies so that they could eat breakfast.

On the other side of the burned district, guardsmen of the Fourth Regiment were also receiving their first meal. The previous evening, commissary officers had begun preparations for feeding the troops. By 4 A.M. the Fourth's commissary unit had procured rations for 250 men from "up town" provision stores. After setting up stationary ranges, they were able to feed 110 men at a time. In order to feed those who had to remain on sentry duty, members of the Fourth Regiment's commissary unit borrowed a hose wagon from the fire department on which they distributed hot coffee, hot sausage, and bread.[17]

Because the fire was still not under control, Fifth Regiment commanders allowed their units little time for breakfast. Some did not eat at all. Of the four companies under Hinkley's command, for example, he relieved the members of B Company briefly, then directed them to relieve L Company. Because the men in companies G and K had been fed by citizens, Hinkley ordered them to remain on the line.[18]

Throughout the morning, however, the sense of urgency surrounding the fire continued to decline. By noon, the fire was confined to the wharf area at the southern end of West Falls Avenue and burned itself out by mid-afternoon. On the west side of the burned district, many Fourth Regiment units began a four hours on/eight hours off rotation. Riggs then reassessed the situation. More guardsmen were required to form a cordon around the 140-acre burned district. To augment the Fourth and Fifth regiments, Riggs activated other units.[19]

That afternoon and evening, in cities and towns across Maryland, companies of the First Regiment boarded trains bound for Baltimore. On leaving Cambridge, members of the First Regiment's Company C were "in high spirits and...expect[ed] to have a good time." As the companies arrived in the city, they marched directly to the Fifth Regiment armory, where the First Regiment was divided into three battalions of four companies each. It was a sound strategy. While two battalions were on guard duty, the third rested. With the exception of the first day's guard assignment, the rotation allowed each battalion to rest 24 hours before its 48-hour duty.[20]

Other elements of brigade strategy involving the First Regiment were not so well thought out. No arrangement had been made to feed the relief units. Instead, brigade officers issued company commanders money and instructed them to "hustle and secure something for their men." Although commanders reported purchasing food such as sandwiches and coffee from nearby stores or restaurants, the daily search became an unwelcome chore.[21]

In addition to calling-up the First Regiment, Riggs activated the Naval Brigade to secure Baltimore's waterfront. A combination of cold winds blowing off the water and a lack of shelter in the wharf area made the navy's

First Regiment mess tent at Fayette Street west of Gay Street. The tents served both enlisted men and officers. Here, three officers (striped pants without leggings) stand among their soldiers. The men, who were reported to be from Annapolis, were members of either Company G or M. (Peale Museum, City Life Museums)

duty the most severe faced by guardsmen. Citizen-sailors, or "jackies," who patrolled the harbor in cutters day and night, were often forced to break through ice with their oars.

Supporting the cutter activity, navy men were headquartered on the USS *Sylvia*, moored at Bowly's Wharf. Motorized vessels borrowed from Baltimore transportation companies were also used by the sailors. Never totalling more than 142 men, naval forces numbered 72 on the eighth, 100 on the ninth, and thereafter averaged 134 until the Naval Brigade was dismissed on the 23rd.[22]

Riggs also called upon the untested Signal Corps to establish and maintain intra-brigade communication. On Tuesday, February ninth, having no tools or equipment of their own, members of the Signal Corps borrowed required materials from the Maryland Telephone Company. Over the next few days the eight-man unit strung lines between the various headquarters, including that of the Naval Brigade at Bowly's Wharf.[23]

The navy line proved the most difficult to maintain because it crossed the heart of the burned district. Few telephone poles in that area had survived the fire; therefore, signalmen were forced to elevate communication lines on "lancepoles," which had to be driven into the frozen ground. Because the makeshift line was subject to high winds and falling bricks, it required frequent repairs, sometimes in the middle of the night.[24]

Navy and Army guardsmen keep watch over clean-up operations. Note the contrast in uniforms. The Naval Brigade enlisted man wears a heavy pea coat and wool gloves and toque that covers his ears. The enlisted soldier appears less comfortable with his collar turned up against the February temperatures. (MSA SC 1890-05-4490)

Another problem for the Signal Corps was the presence of live electric lines within the burned district. After his unit discovered the live wires, the Signal Corps commander detailed a corporal and a first class private to supervise "two gangs of men from the United Co[mpany] who were engaged in salvaging the wire." That work continued until all overhead wires were removed.[25]

"pneumonia was almost certain [to] follow"

Beginning Monday evening, February 8, guardsmen encircling the burned district settled into the dull routine of sentry duty. In addition to those on the perimeter, infantrymen formed a roving guard within the closed zone. Harsh winter weather added to the guardsmen's ordeal. High winds combined with low temperatures kept the wind chill below 15 degrees until

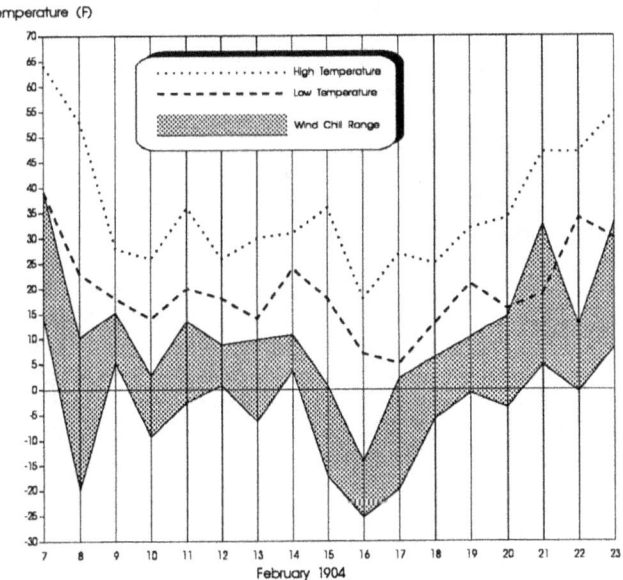

State Weather Service meteorologists at 512 N. Howard Street recorded daily high and low temperatures without reference to the time of day they were measured. On the other hand, they took wind speed readings each day at 8 a.m. and again at 8 p.m. They did not compute wind chill. For the purposes of this book, a wind chill (WC) range for each day was established by averaging the daily wind speeds (W) and then entering the average into the formula WC = T - (1.5W), where T represents both the high and low temperature and W represents the average wind speed. For example, when the WC was figured using T as the high temperature, the upper end of the wind chill range was obtained. Similarly, the low end of the wind chill range was computed using the low temperature for the value of T. Mr. Ken Shaver of the Baltimore Weather Service at the Baltimore Washington International Airport allowed me to copy pertinent weather tables from records maintained there.

the fire. Five-cent cigars were traded for brickbats. Later, after major streets through the burned district were cleared of debris, sentries oversaw pedestrian traffic through the restricted zone. Still others spent long hours preventing people from entering areas where engineers were razing buildings. [31]

Difficulties faced by guardsmen were not limited to sentry duty. The more than 2,000 guardsmen on duty in the city strained available quartering space. Members of the Fourth Regiment were fortunate in that they patrolled the westernmost section of the burned district and were able to sleep in their armory on West Fayette Street. Because members of the Fifth Regiment were posted across the city from their armory on North Howard Street, they had to sleep in the rented Labor Lyceum building on East Baltimore Street. To help relieve the crowded conditions there, city officials offered additional space in the City Morgue. After Captain Jesse Slingluff inspected the available space and found the coroner in the midst of an autopsy, he proclaimed the morgue "uncanny and gruesome." Instead of using the proffered space, Slingluff opted to continue housing his men in the cramped Labor Lyceum quarters. Most members of the First Regiment, meanwhile, slept on borrowed cots in the Post Office. Members of the Naval Brigade slept in a building near the Labor Lyceum as well as on board the vessels *Sylvia* and *Ivanhoe*. Brigade officers slept in a separate area of the Post Office under conditions that were nearly as austere as those of the enlisted men.[32]

National Guard routine did not change significantly until February 15, when Riggs ordered the force reduced; accordingly, the brigade was reorganized into two provisional regiments that Monday. Nine companies of the First Regiment were sent home and soldiers from the three remaining companies were merged with units of the Fourth or Fifth regiments. On February 16, the Fourth Regiment consisted of two battalions of five companies each. Three of the ten companies were manned by First Regiment soldiers. The Fifth Regiment was reduced to a provisional battalion of five companies; reorganized companies ranged in strength from 48 to 65 men each. Beginning February 20, Riggs reduced further the forces under his command. As cleanup efforts progressed, he contracted the sentry lines, thereby opening portions of the burned district to the public.[33]

In a letter to his adjutant general on February 22nd, Governor Edwin Warfield stated that "the time has arrived for the withdrawal of the militia." Warfield's opinion was relayed to the president of the Board of Police Commissioners which relieved the remaining elements of the First Brigade at 6 P.M. the next day. It was probably not a coincidence that guardsmen were withdrawn just thirty-six hours after the termination of a state holiday that had been in effect since February 8. The legal holiday had been declared to aid the owners of destroyed businesses by allowing them time to recover valuables from vaults and to establish temporary places of business. Once this had been accomplished, Baltimore businesses no longer required the holiday or the National Guard sentries. [34]

February 21st. To limit their men's exposure to the cold, officers of the guard relieved sentries every one or two hours. Between shifts, those on perimeter duty took shelter within buildings in space donated by businessmen. Guardsmen on roving patrol rested in the Post Office corridors after every two hours of duty.[26]

Underlying the officers' precautions was the knowledge that their men were poorly equipped for the frigid temperatures. Although protected by wool overcoats and gum ponchos, infantrymen were not issued fur gloves or toques until February 18! Several officers also complained of the poor condition of the uniforms; one declared that the "trousers of several men...were too short, and but for their wearing leggins they would have been unfit for service."[27]

The combination of cold weather and poorly prepared militia compelled Baltimore's Health Commissioner, Dr. James Bosley, to make repeated calls for federal troops to relieve the guard. On February 13, for instance, Bosley informed Mayor McLane that guardsmen were already suffering from "much sickness" caused by long hours in cold temperatures. He warned the mayor, moreover, that "pneumonia was almost certain [to] follow." His statement proved prophetic.[28]

Three enlisted men pose among the ruins. Despite wind chills that rarely rose above 15 degrees, only the soldier carrying a rifles wears an overcoat and gloves; none of the three wear knitted caps or ear protection. (MSA SC 1890-03-4492)

On February 16, Private Joseph Undutch of the Fourth Regiment's Company F fell ill. Five days later, he died of pneumonia at his parents' home. On February 17, illness also struck the Fourth Regiment's Second Lieutenant John V. Richardson of Company E. After being sent home with a temperature of 104 degrees, an army doctor reported that "double pneumonia...developed, which resulted in his death a few hours later." The two soldiers were the only fatalities, military or civilian, that can be directly attributed to the fire.[29]

Sentries eased the discomfort associated with winter duty by constructing shelters from bricks and tin. Most built picket fires, which they burned throughout the night. Although the fires provided welcomed warmth, they were also a source of danger. One night, sentries from a Fourth Regiment company used a sledge hammer to dislodge wood frozen to the floor of a half-burned building. When they returned for more firewood the next day, guardsmen noticed a safe, "supported only by a badly charred rafter," poised immediately above the area from which they had gathered wood the night before.[30]

During the day, guardsmen who kept busy controlling crowds that gathered to view the devastation. Some in the crowd bartered with sentries for relics of

Soldier's shelter. Guardsmen constructed makeshift shelters from materials and debris found within the burnt district. Here, a canvas tarp and sheet of metal serve as a roof for a shelter erected in front of a burned-out building. A city policeman looks over the shoulders of an officer (on left with saber) and an enlisted guardsman. (Peale Museum, City Life Museums)

Baltimore's central business district before the fire, ca. 1903. The fire spread quickly through this area of crowded buildings and narrow streets. The Merchant's National Bank Building, situated at the southeast corner of Water and South streets, is the large building in the center. Wagons (center right) parked on Exchange Place between South and Commerce streets. (MSA SC 2796-03-99)

The same section of Baltimore's central business district after the fire. The southwestern corner of the Merchant's National Bank Building can be seen in the upper left. (MSA SC 1890-03-4-489)

The Labor Lyceum located at 1011 East Baltimore Street, ca. 1905. Situated just three blocks east of the Jones Falls, over four hundred Fifth Regiment guardsmen lived in this hall from February 8-23. (Peale Museum, Baltimore City Life Museums)

"MIGHTY IS RIGGS!"

The guard's presence in Baltimore had a political dimension that involved the local, state, and even the federal governments. On February 8, to limit the possibility of looting or injury, municipal and military authorities restricted access to the burned district to those who had been issued passes. Only persons with legitimate business interests inside the burnt district were issued a pass. Accountability for those passing through the lines fell to the guardsmen. It proved to be a thankless task.

Since several agencies issued passes, sentries encountered permits signed variously by the mayor, the police commissioner, the governor, or brigade officers. Further complicating their duty were attempts to breach the lines by persons who presented fraudulent passes. In one such instance, a man claiming to be a newspaper reporter flashed a badge at an inquiring sentry. Upon closer inspection, however, the purported badge proved to be "last years dog license tag sewn on his vest." Similarly, a young woman waved her pass at a sentry as she hurried through the line. Suspicious, the guard stopped her and found that her pass was actually a medical prescription written in Latin. [35]

In addition to confusion prompted by multiple and spurious passes, guardsmen received inconsistent orders regarding burned district restrictions. For example, a Fourth Regiment officer reported that only firemen with a badge and those with passes from the mayor, police, or regimental or brigade headquarters were allowed through the lines. At the same time in another part of the burned district, a First Regiment unit allowed uniformed firemen with a badge, uniformed police, the Fire Marshal, city street cleaning crews, and newspaper reporters to pass through their lines. Still others were allowed into the burned district without passes. Guarding the Merchant & Miners Transportation Company's wharf, sentries allowed only those who could be identified as employees to pass through the line. Another unit guarding the area near the Fidelity, Trust & Deposit Company, of which Governor Warfield was president, was ordered to "allow only those having business in the Fidelity building to pass." Later, the unit commander complained that his men "found it very trying and at times almost impossible to distinguish who had business and who had not."[36]

Guardsmen were not the only group annoyed by the pass system. The city's leading bankers and businessmen had to stand in lines to receive passes. "A great many," reported the *Sun*, "complained bitterly" about having to obtain a pass to visit their former places of business. The paper assured its readers, however, that all those who had "legitimate business within the fire lines were accommodated." The *Sun* declared that the pass system was "necessary in order to protect property."[37]

Within twenty-four hours of its introduction, however, authorities realized that the multiple pass system was unworkable. On the morning of February 9, therefore, state, municipal, and military representatives met in Baltimore to discuss a new strategy. They decided that the Board of Police Commissioners would have sole approval authority over passes and that all passes would be issued by Brigadier General Riggs, who would assume full responsibility for the security of the burned district. Furthermore, the group invalidated all passes issued under the initial, day-old system. These decisions immediately met with a negative response.

The *Sun* now complained that Riggs refused to issue passes to newspaper reporters. Withholding the passes, declared the *Sun*, "doubled the already difficult work of the newspaper men." It was not the only paper to complain about pass restrictions. An Annapolis newspaper asked sarcastically, "Would not Generalissimo Riggs feel pretty bad if there were no newspapers to report his greatness?"[38]

The newspapers had a legitimate grievance. Riggs obstructed the distribution of passes at every turn. For example, when Baltimore City State's Attorney Albert S. J. Owens tried to intercede on behalf of the reporters, Riggs refused to meet with him. Only after Mayor McLane intervened did Riggs reluctantly agree to issue five passes to each paper. When newspaper publishers protested that five passes were not enough and demanded more, Riggs would not relent. Instead, he affirmed his policy of keeping the burned district "as free from pedestrians as possible."[39]

Guards hold back crowd in front of 16 East Lexington Street. While his soldiers manned the perimeter, an officer (lower left with saber) eyes the crowd. Spectators, including several women, reflect a variety of social and ethnic origins. (MSA SC 1890-03-4639)

Riggs's determination to limit non-essential access to the burned area was not based on whimsy. By pedestrians, Riggs meant any non-guardsmen. Already policemen, firemen, building inspectors, work crews, and city officials of various descriptions roamed the burned district. Riggs was responsible for all of them as well as the property within the closed zone. He was also accountable for the lives and actions of the over 2,000 guardsmen who patrolled the district. Their lack of experience must have informed Riggs's exclusionary strategy. The majority of his men had less than three years national guard experience. On February 23, subsequent to praising his men, Riggs added a revealing personal postscript. "So far as I am concerned," he declared, "I am very glad to be relieved of the responsibility...[of protecting] the lives and property of the residents and business public of Baltimore." [40]

That no one was exempted from Riggs's exclusionary policy was made more obvious when in the General Assembly Delegate Walter A. Johnson introduced a resolution condemning Riggs for refusing to honor passes signed by the governor, which had been issued to members of the House of Delegates. Johnson's resolution passed with an amendment that ordered Riggs to appear before the House at noon the next day, February 11, to explain the Guard's conduct. The nature of the House action was both political and personal. House Democrats maintained that by refusing to honor their passes, Riggs had insulted Democratic Governor Warfield. At the same time, members' comments revealed their individual outrage at being turned away by guardsmen. Whatever their motivation, House members overwhelmingly supported the resolution. Although no vote was recorded, a related resolution to pay the House sergeant-at-arms $25 for mileage and expenses incurred while summoning Riggs passed the House by 84 votes to three.[41]

Recognizing an ally in the House membership, the *Sun* escalated its attack on the general. "MIGHTY IS RIGGS!" exclaimed the headline over its article that alleged (erroneously) that, among other things, Riggs had usurped the Constitution and established "a de facto state of martial law." In a prominent editorial, the newspaper compared Riggs to Dogberry, the absurd and blundering constable in Shakespeare's *Much Ado About Nothing*. Juxtaposed with its attack on Riggs's character, the *Sun* applauded the legislature's condemnation of the general's actions. If the House of Delegates was going to embarrass Riggs, the newspaper must have believed, so much the better for the press.[42]

The next day, however, instead of embarrassing Riggs the House voted to reconsider and expunge its *Journal* record of the resolution that had ordered him before the bar. The settlement was orchestrated by Governor Warfield. About an hour before appearing in front of the House, Riggs met with Delegate Johnson, Senate President Spencer Cone Jones, House Speaker George Y. Everhart, and Warfield in the governor's mansion. During that meeting, the politicians reached a compromise. Apparently, Johnson agreed to recant his previous statements about Riggs in return for a more liberal policy regarding the general's distribution of passes. The *Sun* labeled the compromise a "whitewash," but because the press had achieved its goal of greater access to passes, Riggs and the pass issue disappeared from the headlines.[43]

While the controversy over the issuing of passes into the burned-out area was resolved quickly, it may have been symptomatic of deeper political divisions within the state. Democratic governor Edwin Warfield, inaugurated only two weeks before the Baltimore Fire, had run for and won election against Arthur Pue Gorman's powerful Democratic machine. The actions of the machine-controlled General Assembly in the immediate post-fire crisis illustrated the tension between Gorman and Warfield.[44]

Despite its claim that Riggs had insulted the governor by refusing to honor passes signed by Warfield, it seems likely that when the House on February 10 ordered Riggs to appear before it the following day the House intended by its quick and nearly unanimous action to chasten and embarrass the renegade Democratic governor. Another resolution passed by the assembly on that same day, February 10, tends to confirm the suggestion. This resolution called on President Theodore Roosevelt "to direct the Secretary of War to dispatch United States Troops to Baltimore City."[45]

As with the pass controversy, powerful public support was quickly marshalled in support of the Assembly's call for federal intervention. On February 11, Charles C. Homer, president of the Clearinghouse Association, an organization of Baltimore financial leaders, sent a telegram to Secretary of War William Howard Taft, asking him to "instruct the Commander of the United States troops detailed to guard the [U.S. Post Office and U.S. Custom House] to furnish escorts" to safeguard funds being transported to and from the Custom House.[46]

The Assembly's request to the president for federal troops, bolstered by the private Clearinghouse Association's plea for aid to the secretary of war, implied that Maryland's chief executive and its state military were incapable of handling the crisis caused by the Baltimore Fire. Warfield would have none of it. He signed the resolution and dispatched Adjutant General Clinton L. Riggs, brother of Brigadier General Lawrason Riggs, to deliver it to Roosevelt. But Maryland's Adjutant General also carried a statement from Governor Warfield that assured Roosevelt that federal troops were not needed in Baltimore and informing him that if the president sent them he, Warfield, "would at once request their withdrawal." [47]

Secretary of War Taft, who refused to be drawn into the fray, responded to the Clearinghouse Association's request by citing his constitutional inability to order federal troops to the area. Roosevelt responded on Friday. Citing provisions within Title 69, section 5297, governing the use of federal troops to suppress local disturbances, Roosevelt concluded that in the absence of "domestic violence or insurrection," no requirement for federal troops existed. He declined, therefore, to comply with the legislature's resolution and with the exception of demolition engineers, federal troops were never sent to Baltimore.[48]

"I was deeply impressed with the elegance of the Atheneum."

The political sparring caused by the Great Fire of 1904 had no impact on the more than 2,000 guardsmen on the line. They continued day after day under arduous conditions to comport themselves responsibly and professionally. This was not the result of rigorous military training—most guardsmen were recent recruits and training was largely limited to summer encampments—but rather a reflection of the organization and composition of the guard itself.

The public image of the post-Civil War Guard is that it was little more than a social club, with rigid class lines based on socio-economic lines. Most Guard units that served at the fire, however, were generally democratic. Officers and enlisted men from all walks of life worked and lived together during the emergency. While on guard duty, privates, noncommissioned officers, and line officers were equally exposed to the February temperatures. Relief quarters, moreover, often housed both officers and enlisted

Going on guard duty. A national guard platoon, probably from the Fifth Regiment, marches across the East Baltimore Street bridge over the Jones Falls. The Monumental Bowling Alleys, which did not burn, can be seen in the background. (Stephen A. Goldman Collection, MSA SC 3493-1-1).

men. Brigadier General Riggs and his staff slept in the Post Office along with the members of the First Regiment.[49]

Throughout its fire service, the Guard's tradition of electing its officers continued. In one instance, a sergeant was elected second lieutenant, but that was not the only time the men were polled. Before the provisional regiments were formed on February 15, one company commander recalled being "ordered to ascertain the feelings of my men as to continuing on duty."[50]

Furthermore, some officers expressed an intimate knowledge of their men. When Second Lieutenant E. O. Streett reported for duty on February 7, he was ordered to go to the homes of those in his unit who had not yet reported. He was able to comply with the order because he had the addresses "in his pocket." In his report to the adjutant general, Captain Harvey L. Jones praised fourteen members of his company by name, all of whom were enlisted men.[51]

Mounted officer addresses guardsman standing at port arms. The officer is probably a member of the brigade staff, which along with Troop A, used horses during the fire service. (MSA SC 1890-03-4491)

Despite the democratic nature of most companies within the First Brigade, however, its lone cavalry unit, Troop A, epitomized the elite qualities often associated with the Maryland National Guard of the post-Civil War era. Purposefully reminiscent of the Confederacy, the 45-man unit drilled on the grounds of the Confederate Home for the Aged in Towson. By 1904, however, such elitism was anachronistic.[52]

Formed in 1896, Troop A was an exclusive unit. Each member was required to furnish his own horse. Unlike members of the infantry units, Troop A personnel were employed primarily in high white collar or white collar occupations. Among the eighteen privates whose occupation could be identified, one was a physician, two were lawyers, and seven were clerks. Only one, a tanner, held a skilled-labor job; none were unskilled.[53]

The high socio-economic status of Troop A members translated into favorable treatment during the Baltimore duty. Cavalrymen were used primarily as pickets to prevent people from straying into areas where engineers were dynamiting buildings. Since blasting operations were suspended by eight o'clock every night, Troop A members had the distinction of being the only guardsmen not required to perform duty twenty-four hours a day.

Moreover, while most infantrymen were quartered in crowded corridors, rented halls, or armories, cavalry troops slept comfortably in a vacated nurses' dormitory at the City Hospital. Instead of eating food prepared or delivered by a brigade commissary, members of Troop A dined at the Athenaeum Club, which counted among its select clientele President Roosevelt. The amenities available to the members of Troop A apparently left lasting impressions on at least one soldier. Fifty years later, a former cavalryman recalled that "Despite the gravity of the Fire,...I was deeply impressed with the elegance of the Atheneum."[54]

"... will reflect great credit and honor upon the State of Maryland"[55]

Although most histories of Baltimore include sections about the Great Fire, the Maryland National Guard's role during the fire and its aftermath has been under-reported and its presence often reduced to photograph captions. Histories of the fire, however, are incomplete without an examination of the more than 2,000 guardsmen who patrolled the burned district for seventeen days.

Called out to protect property and to prevent looting, guardsmen had to overcome a myriad of obstacles. Delayed initially by an unorganized command, once in the field guardsmen encountered reluctant saloon patrons as well as large and determined crowds of spectators. Guardsmen were further plagued by inadequate equipment, sub-zero temperatures, forty-eight-hour duties, and improvised eating and sleeping arrangements. Despite these and other problems, guardsmen fulfilled their mandate diligently.

The seventeen-day service at the Great Baltimore Fire had a profound effect on the Maryland National Guard. Guard officials realized that holiday parades and summer encampments had not prepared it for the emergency call-up. In the weeks and months following the fire, officers and enlisted men worked to professionalize the state military. Armories were redesigned and remodeled to allow better access to supplies and to avoid the costly delays experienced on February 7 and 8.

Moreover, its success at the fire helped to alter the prevailing "social club" image that many in Maryland had of the Guard. People now understood that guardsmen were no longer simply former Confederates who enjoyed parading in smart grey uniforms. Instead, guardsmen represented a cross-section of a rapidly modernizing and urbanizing state. Most were no longer attracted to the Guard as a way of perpetuating the memory of the Lost Cause, but rather as a way of serving their fellow citizens. And the Baltimore Fire of 1904 made clear to those very citizens just how important an organized Guard was in the modern world. Urban sprawl and congestion meant that civil emergencies would inexorably be part of the twentieth century. The Guard's actions at the Great Baltimore Fire of 1904 and its aftermath illustrated that Maryland had the citizen soldiers to respond.

Notes

1. Christine Meisner Rosen, *The Limits of Power, Great Fires and the Process of City Growth in America* (New York: Cambridge University Press, 1986), p. 249.

2. At the time of the fire, German Street (renamed Redwood Street during World War I), extended through what is now Hopkins Plaza. The Hurst Building was located in the vicinity of what is now the Baltimore Civic Center. Received in Washington, D.C., at 11:40 A.M., Horton's telegram read: "Desperate fire here. Must have help at once." Quoted in Harold A. Williams, *Baltimore Afire* (Baltimore: Schneidereith & Sons, 1954), p. 5.

3. At 8 P.M., a Johns Hopkins' weather station located at 512 North Howard Street measured the southwest wind at 24 mph, with gusts to 32 mph.

4. *Annual Report of the Adjutant General* of Maryland, 1904-1905 (Baltimore: King Bros., State Printers, 1906), p. 10. The Baltimore City Board of Police Commissioners or any county sheriff was authorized to call out the National Guard "to aid in preventing threatened disorder or opposition to the laws, or in suppressing riots or disorder" (*Laws of 1896*, ch. 89, art. xxxiv). The law, moreover, subordinated the National Guard Commander to local civilian authority. In the case of the Baltimore Fire, Brigadier General Lawrason Riggs was subordinate to the Board of Police Commissioners. Only the Governor could countermand its orders. As a result, the Adjutant General was excluded from the command structure. Throughout its fire service, First Brigade Headquarters remained at Fayette and Calvert streets, though not always within the City Hall building. When fire threatened the City Hall at about ten o'clock Sunday night, Riggs established a temporary headquarters in Gaspari's Tobacco Store, located at 205 N. Calvert Street at the rear of the Metropolitan Savings Bank.

5. Lieutenant Colonel J. Frank Supplee, Fourth Regiment Executive Officer, dispatched one of his men to request that the mayor have the riot call rung on the City Hall bell. Supplee reported that Mayor Robert McLane telephoned him, inquiring as to the riot call procedure. After Supplee told McLane that the riot call was "three three's rung about six times," McLane reportedly climbed into the belfry and rang the bell. Report of Lieutenant Colonel Supplee, February 20, 1904, ADJUTANT GENERAL (Baltimore Fire Papers) [MSA S 956, MdHR 50,077-1](hereafter cited as Baltimore Fire Papers); and "How Mayor M'Lane Rang the Riot Call," Baltimore *American*, February 17, 1904, p. 2.

6. Reports of Colonel Henry Warfield and First Lieutenant W. Pinkney Holmes, Baltimore Fire Papers.

7. Reports of Lieutenant Colonel Supplee, February 20, 1904, and Major D. F. Pennington, Baltimore Fire Papers. Pennington wrote that when he arrived about 9:30 P.M., he found "Enlisted Men helping themselves to Overcoats, Canteens, Haversacks, [and] Blankets," and report of Captain George F. Haupt, Baltimore Fire Papers.

8. Reports of Captain Bruce B. Gootee, First Lieutenant Asa L. Wessels, and Captain J. Clifton Keyes, Baltimore Fire Papers.

9   Reports of Lieutenant Colonel Supplee, February 21, 1904, and First Lieutenant J. E. Rittenhouse, Baltimore Fire Papers. At the port arms position, the rifle is held centered in front of the body with the bayonet pointing upward.

10 Report of Major Harry C. Jones, Baltimore Fire Papers. A search of newspaper accounts of the early hours of the Fourth Regiment's guard duty failed to uncover any account of bayoneted horses.

11 Reports of Second Lieutenant James P. Houstoun and First Lieutenant S. E. Conradt, Baltimore Fire Papers. Many Fifth Regiment officers reported having to confront intoxicated citizens in the vicinity of the Jones Falls. Company B commander, Captain Thomas S. Janney, wrote that drunken men had been enticed to saloons "where free drinks were being dispensed." Baltimore Fire Papers.

12 Reports of Major John Hinkley and Captain Gootee, Baltimore Fire Papers. No one named Bokee was listed on any brigade payroll. Therefore, "Capt. Bokee" was probably Captain Bruce B. Gootee, commander of Company H, Fourth Regiment. Gootee reported moving crowds back to Baltimore and Exeter streets and being relieved at 4 A.M. by elements of the Fifth Regiment. Beginning from its post at South and Baltimore streets, Gootee's unit was probably forced eastward as shifting winds drove the fire toward them from the northwest.

13 Reports of Second Lieutenant Upton S. Brady and Major Hinkley. Hinkley reported that "no cartridges were issued to the troops" under his command. Baltimore Fire Papers.

14 Report of Colonel Warfield, Baltimore Fire Papers.

15 Baltimore *American*, February 15, 1904, p. 1; and the *Afro-American Ledger*, February 13, 1904, p. 1.

16 Reports of Major Hinkley and First Lieutenant W. Spear Brownley, Baltimore Fire Papers.

17 Report of Captain Lester Kingsbury, Baltimore Fire Papers. Many reports also acknowledged numerous Baltimoreans who provided guardsmen with meals throughout the seventeen-day duty. Some, the officers reported, supplied sentries with hot coffee 24 hours a day.

18 Companies B, G, K, and L comprised Hinkley's regular battalion. Companies A and E had been reassigned to their proper battalion between the hours of 2 and 5 A.M.

19 In his annual report, the Baltimore Fire Chief stated that the "conflagration raged until 11:30 A.M." *Annual Report of the Board of Fire Commissioners for 1904* (Baltimore: Wm. J. C. Dulany Company, 1904), p. 18.

20 Companies that formed the First Regiment were located in Cumberland, Hagerstown, Cambridge, Bel Air, Elkton, Easton, Salisbury, Rockville, Centreville, Westminster, and Annapolis. The enthusiastic men were described in the Cambridge *Democrat & News*, February 13, 1904, p. 3. None of the railroads charged a fee for transporting the guardsmen.

21 Reports of First Lieutenant George R. Tydings, First Lieutenant Joseph M. Parvis, and Captain Phil E. Porter, among others, Baltimore Fire Papers. In an appropriate characterization, Porter reported having to "forage" for rations. Prob-

ably as a result of complaints from the First Regiment, beginning on February 11, mess tents and portable ovens were provided each company. Units were also issued a per diem, based on company strength, with which to purchase food, wood, and cooks' labor. Thereafter, except for the Fourth, regimental commissaries were discontinued.

22 Letter to the paymaster from the Adjutant General, June 4, 1904. ADJUTANT GENERAL (Miscellaneous Papers) 1904 [MSA S927, MdHR 50,056-159]. Although a memorandum to the Adjutant General from the Chief Paymaster dated July 1, 1904, indicated that the Naval Brigade payroll had been forwarded by "First Class postage," no payrolls are included within the documents held by the Maryland State Archives. ADJUTANT GENERAL (Baltimore Fire Papers) [MSA S956, MdHR 50,077-1]. Nor are there any officer reports within that record group. A search of the Fifth Regiment archives situated within the North Howard Street armory also failed to locate the desired documents. Less detailed information is contained in the *Annual Report of the Adjutant General of Maryland, 1904-1905*, p. 224 and in the Baltimore *Sun*, February 26, 1904, p. 8. Bowly's Wharf was sometimes referred to as "Bowley's Wharf." A map of Baltimore in 1896 spells it "Bowlys Wharf." Edward C. Papenfuse and Joseph M. Coale, III, *Atlas of Historical Maps of Maryland, 1608-1908* (Baltimore: Johns Hopkins University Press, 1982), p. 112.

23 Report of First Lieutenant Sydney B. Austin, Signal Corps Commander, Baltimore Fire Papers. In an 1897 report, the Adjutant General called for the establishment of a Signal Corps, but subsequent reports make no mention of how or when it was organized. *Annual Report of the Adjutant General, 1897* (Baltimore: King Bros., 1898), p. 5. In 1898, the Signal Corps was comprised of one officer and eight enlisted men, *Annual Report of the Adjutant General, 1900* (Baltimore: Wm. J. C. Dulany Company, State Printers, 1900), p. 100.

24 Report of Lieutenant Austin, Baltimore Fire Papers.

25 Ibid. The United Company to which Austin referred may have been the United Railways and Electric Company. After its offices were destroyed by the fire, UR&E established a temporary office in the Maryland Telephone Building.

26 Reports of Second Lieutenant French S. Carey, Captain Albert S. Gill, and Captain Moumonier Rowe, Baltimore Fire Papers; see also the Baltimore *News*, February 10, 1904, p. 2. Although several officers reported taking refuge in buildings offered by businessmen, in at least one case guardsmen had to "pile their equipment" on the sidewalk outside while they warmed themselves in a retail store that continued to carry on business around them. Report of Captain Phil E. Porter, Baltimore Fire Papers.

27 Reports of First Lieutenant Holmes and Second Lieutenant F. Louck, Baltimore Fire Papers. In addition to the gloves and toques, the Brigade Quartermaster ordered 1,606 pairs of shoes and 590 blankets. Baltimore *News*, February 13, 1904, p. 12. Additionally, First Lieutenant J. Frank Ryley reported that a few Baltimore businesses contributed "about 1,000 pairs of good gloves."

28 *American*, February 14, 1904, p. 2.

29 Report of Captain W. Guy Townsend, Baltimore Fire Papers. While Harold A. Williams's account of the fire mentions a contemporary rumor that one man

drowned trying to escape the flames, Williams reports the account seems to be without foundation, *Baltimore Afire*, p. 43. Other historical works that concentrate on the fire or Baltimore's reconstruction have overlooked the deaths related to the fire's aftermath. For example, "no one was killed," in Suzanne Ellery Greene, *An Illustrated History of Baltimore* (Woodland Hills, CA: Windsor Publications, Inc., 1980), p. 174, and "but there were no deaths," in Sherry H. Olson, *Baltimore, the Building of an American City* (Baltimore: Johns Hopkins University, 1980), p. 247.

30 Report of Charles K. Duce, Baltimore Fire Papers.

31 Captain Gootee was told that some souvenirs were sent to the mayors of Chicago, San Francisco, Jacksonville, and London, Baltimore Fire Papers. The rate of exchange was reported in the Baltimore *American*, February 15, 1904, p. 2.

32 Report of Captain Jesse Slingluff, Baltimore Fire Papers. Some officers referred to the Labor Lyceum as the Carroll Hall. The building was located at 1011 East Baltimore Street.

33 The Naval Brigade maintained its separate command structure and was not reduced.

34 Warfield's letter is in the ADJUTANT GENERAL (Miscellaneous Papers) [MSA S927, MdHR 50,056-159]. Upshur's letter to Brigadier General Lawrason Riggs was published in the *Report of the Board of Police Commissioners for the City of Baltimore: 1904-1905* (Baltimore: Wm. J. C. Dulany Company, 1906) p. 15. For information on the legal holidays see the *Laws of 1904*, chapter 1, and GOVERNOR (Proceedings), p. 47 [MSA S1072, MdHR 7902]. For the relationship between the state holiday and the Clearinghouse Association, see ibid, pp. 49-50.

35 Reports of Second Lieutenants French S. Carey and Charles K. Duce, Baltimore Fire Papers.

36 Reports of First Lieutenant E. H. Gaither, Captain L. P. Coulbourn, First Lieutenant Gustave W. Ridgely, and Captain Moumonier Rowe, Baltimore Fire Papers. Throughout the crisis, Governor Warfield used his Fidelity office as a Baltimore executive headquarters and was probably in the building when Rowe was ordered to guard it.

37 Baltimore *Sun*, February 9, 1904, p. 6, and the Baltimore *American*, February 9, 1904, p. 1.

38 Baltimore *Sun*, February 10, 1904, p. 6, and Annapolis *Evening Capital*, February 11, 1904, p. 2.

39 Baltimore *Sun*, February 11, 1904, p. 16.

40 Baltimore *American*, February 24, 1904, p. 2. Data indicate that about 80 percent of guardsmen who served at the fire had fewer than four years' national guard experience. Statistical tables available at the Maryland State Archives in TOPIC FILE [MSA G 1456-1907, 0/70/9/20].

41 *Journal of Proceedings of the House of Delegates of Maryland, 1904*, (Annapolis: Wm. J. C. Dulany Company, 1904), p. 259, pp. 345-346. Governor Warfield had issued passes to House members in response to House Resolution no. 1, which was passed on February 8, 1904, Ibid, p. 237. See also GOVERNOR (Pro-

ceedings), p. 48, [MSA S1072, MdHR 7902]. On February 11, Johnson reportedly announced that when he sponsored the resolution, "he was convinced that the members of the House had been the victims of a discourteous attack." Baltimore *Sun*, February 12, 1904, p. 12.

42 Baltimore *Sun*, February 11, 1904, p. 16.

43 Ibid., February 12, 1904, p. 12. On the 10th, Governor Warfield asked his Attorney General, William S. Bryan, Jr., his opinion whether Riggs should appear at the bar of the House of Delegates. Bryan responded the same day. Grounding his opinion in the Constitution, Bryan asserted that the House could not require Riggs or anyone else to testify against himself. Moreover, nothing in Riggs's conduct, Bryan wrote, could be construed as "disrespectful or disorderly behavior in [the House] presence or for obstructing any of [House] proceedings or any of its officers in the exercise of any duty." In conclusion Bryan added that "it shall be the duty of the said military force [when called out by the Board of Police Commissioners] to obey such orders as may be given them by said Board." GOVERNOR (Attorney General Opinions) [MSA S1043, MdHR 5394-1]. Indeed, the next day when Riggs was asked by a delegate if he would now honor a legislator's pass signed by the governor, the general replied that "If the Board of Police Commissioners ordered me to do so I would." Baltimore *Sun*, February 12, 1904, p. 12. The day after Riggs testified before the House, Colonel Charles D. Gaither, whom Riggs had put in charge of issuing passes, "listened to several thousand applicants, and granted many passes." Baltimore *American*, February 12, 1904, p. 1.

44 While the animosity between Warfield and Gorman has been traced to Warfield's failed attempt to win the Democratic gubernatorial nomination in 1899, maneuvers by the General Assembly and Governor Warfield during the fire crisis foreshadowed the March 1904 split within the Democratic party over a constitutional amendment to disfranchise black voters. In March, Governor Warfield's public stand against the disfranchisement of tax-paying black citizens "completed the break between [him] and his party organization." Frank R. Kent, *The Story of Maryland Politics* (Hatboro, PA: Traditional Press, 1968), 332. See also Frank F. White, Jr., *The Governors of Maryland 1777-1970* (Annapolis: Hall of Records Commission, 1970), 233-236. For information on Warfield and black disfranchisement, see Margaret Law Callcott, *The Negro in Maryland Politics 1870-1912* (Baltimore: Johns Hopkins Press, 1969), 102-125.

45 The joint resolution passed the House 82 to 3 and the Senate unanimously. *Journal of Proceedings of the House of Delegates of Maryland, 1904* (Annapolis: Wm. J. C. Dulany Company, 1904), pp. 268-270, and *Journal of Proceedings of the Senate of Maryland, 1904* (Annapolis: Wm. J. C. Dulany Company, 1904), pp. 238-239. The joint resolution and Roosevelt's response are printed in the *House Journal* on pages 312-316.

46 Homer's telegram is mentioned in the Baltimore *American*, February 12, 1904, p.1. Baltimore financial leaders established a sub-treasury within the Custom House in which to store money and other securities salvaged from vaults in the ruins. After a financial company established a temporary office outside the burned district, money had to be transported between it and the Custom House at least twice a day. See also the Baltimore *Sun*, February 11, 1904, p. 16. Both telegrams are in the National Archives, RG 94, Records of the Adjutant General's

Office (Main Correspondence File, 1890-1917) File #518834 (add'l V), Box 3610.

47 By calling out the national guard, the Board of Police Commissioners eliminated the Adjutant General from any direct responsibility for guard actions within the burned district. He was, therefore, available to travel to Washington. Governor Warfield's in ability to out-maneuver Gorman Democrats' attempts to have federal troops replace Maryland guardsmen must have been interpreted as a defeat by machine politicians. In a contemporary history of the Maryland General Assembly, Elihu S. Riley, a Democratic apologist, chronicles the Riggs situation but avoids mentioning the legislature's resolution addressed to President Roosevelt. Elihu S. Riley, *A History of the General Assembly of Maryland 1635-1904* (Baltimore: Nunn & Company, 1905), pp. 417-418.

48 Theodore Roosevelt to Edwin Warfield, February 12, 1904, GOVERNOR (Reports and Investigations) [MSA S1044, MdHR 8075-5]. The Clearinghouse Association was probably instrumental in having legislation passed that established a state holiday for the first week following the fire. *Laws of 1904*, chapter 1. Moreover, upon the association's request Warfield extended the holiday through the 21st. See GOVERNOR (Proceedings), pp. 49-50 [MSA S1072, MdHR 7902]. On February 8, a unit of demolition engineers from the Washington Barracks was dispatched to Baltimore to "aid in controlling the fire." Mayor McLane, however, declined the engineers' offer of assistance and the unit returned to Washington that same evening. Major Edward Burr, US Corps of Engineers, to the United States Adjutant General, February 9, 1904, National Archives, RG 94, Records of the Adjutant General's Office (Main Correspondence File, 1890-1917) File #518834 (add'l V), Box 3610.

49 A statistical study of the members of the Fourth and Fifth regiments indicated that more than 80 percent of privates and 90 percent of NCOs held either skilled or white collar occupations. While guardsmen were more apt to be clerks, lawyers, and physicians, they were also more apt to be confectioners, electricians, machinists, plumbers, or tinners than all white male workers in Baltimore. Overall, guardsmen worked in a wide range of occupations not unlike the diversity of jobs held by their white male civilian counterparts. Statistical tables available at the Maryland State Archives in TOPIC FILE [MSA G 1456-1907, 0/70/9/20].

50 Reports of Captain Harvey L. Jones, Captain Hugh R. Riley, and Captain G. F. Haupt, Baltimore Fire Papers.

51 Reports of Second Lieutenant E. O. Streett and Captain Harvey L. Jones, Baltimore Fire Papers.

52 Late nineteenth century Fifth Regiment parade uniforms, for example, were so much like the uniforms of the Confederate Army "as to excite remark in those days when the ashes had not gathered over the fire kindled by the civil strife." George A. Meekins, *Fifth Regiment, Infantry, Maryland National Guard* (Baltimore: A. Hoen & Co., 1899), p. 28. For other guard connections with the Confederacy, see ibid.

53 *Annual Report of the Adjutant General, 1897*, (Baltimore: King Bros., State Printers, 1898), p. 5; and a newspaper described Troop A member Corporal Robert Garrett, as "one of the wealthiest and most prominent young men in Baltimore." Baltimore *American*, February 15, 1904, p. 2; Statistics and occupational defini-

tions are in the Maryland State Archives TOPIC FILE [MSA G 1456-1907, 0/70/9/20].

54 Harold Curry Hann, *Well Do I Remember: Memories of Old Baltimore* (Baltimore: n.p., 1953), pp. 17, 25, and 37. Hann, a private during the fire, was secretary to the president of the United Railways and Electric Company.

55 Report of Lieutenant Holmes describing the men under his command, Baltimore Fire Papers. Many of the reports included praise of their men and pride in the service they had provided Baltimore and its citizens.

ABBREVIATIONS

BDE	Brigade
BG	Brigadier General
CDR	Commander
CIV	Civilian
COL	Colonel
CPL	Corporal
CPT	Captain
ENS	Ensign
LCR	Lieutenant Commander
LT	Lieutenant
LTC	Lieutenant Colonel
LTJ	Lieutenant Junior Grade
MAJ	Major
PVT	Private
QM	Quartermaster
SGM	Sergeant Major
SGT	Sergeant
1LT	First Lieutenant
1SG	First Sergeant
2LT	Second Lieutenant

ARMY AND NAVY RANKS

Rank is listed in descending order, from highest to lowest rank.

ARMY RANKS*	NAVY RANKS**
Brigadier General	Commander
Colonel	Lieutenant Commander
Lieutenant Colonel	Lieutenant
Major	Lieutenant Junior Grade
Captain	Ensign
First Lieutenant	
Second Lieutenant	
Sergeant Major	
First Sergeant	
Sergeant	
Corporal	
Private	

*Surgeons and Quartermasters did not have associated rank. Some Lieutenants were listed without a "First" or "Second" denotation.

**Navy roster includes officers only.

Roster of Guardsmen Who Served at the Great Fire

The following roster lists 1,879 guardsmen from the First Brigade, Maryland National Guard who served at the Great Baltimore Fire between February seventh and twenty-third, 1904. Thirty-five civilians employed by units as cooks and laborers are also listed.* Right column below indicates total Maryland National Guard time in service in year(s)/month(s).

First Brigade, Maryland National Guard

Brigade Headquarters and Staff

BG	Riggs, Lawrason	Brigade Commander.	07/11
COL	Macklin, C. F.	Brigade Executive Officer.	03/00
COL	Finney, J. M. T.	Listed on Payroll but not paid.	05/11
COL	McLane, Allan	Listed on payroll but not paid. Total service not listed.	
COL	Gaither, Charles D.	Confederate veteran brought out of retirement by BG Riggs to serve as the First Brigade Adjutant General during its fire service. On 11 FEB, Riggs placed Gaither in charge of issuing passes into the burned district.	10/00
MAJ	Starkloff, C. V.	Served 16 days at fire and 25 days "extra duty."	14/00
MAJ	Coale, F. W.		19/00
MAJ	Spence, C. R.		09/09
MAJ	Fort, S. J.	Brigade Ordnance Officer.	01/05
CPT	Shirley, Joseph W.		06/02
LT	Woodside, E. L.	Served 17 days at fire and 5 days "extra duty." Aide-de-camp to BG Riggs.	02/08
LT	Cockey, W. B.		03/00
SGM	Griffith, J. Milton	Brigade Sergeant Major. Acted as BG Riggs' chief clerk.	10/00
1SG	Barrett, Henry S.	Reenlisted during fire service. At time of reenlistment Barrett had a combined 10 years in the US Army and MNG. Served in Fifth Regiment F Company during the Spanish-American War.	09/00
SGT	Cadwell, Charles C.		11/00
SGT	Richardson, J. Newman		01/04

---

* Most roster information was extracted from unit payrolls and officer reports. Because no payrolls or reports from the Naval Brigade were found, naval information was gleaned primarily from newspaper articles and annual reports. See especially, the Baltimore *Sun*, February 26, 1904, p. 8.

SGT	Marshall, J. C.	Brigade Quartermaster Sergeant.	04/00
SGT	Dunlap, James R.	Commissary Sergeant. Total service not listed.	
SGT	Kasemeyer, George W.	Ordnance Sergeant.	21/07
CPL	Reynolds, Clarence	Served 15 days at the fire and 15 days "extra duty." May have worked under MAJ Starkloff as a payroll clerk.	04/09
PVT	Ray, Guy		01/08

First Regiment, Infantry

Headquarters and Staff

COL	Little, Charles A.	Regimental Commander.	17/00
MAJ	Porter, James C.		21/00
MAJ	Purnell, William G.		21/00
MAJ	Claude, W. C.		21/00
MAJ	Wright, William A.		21/00
CPT	Riggs, Samuel of R.		05/10
CPT	Alvey, Charles		05/10
CPT	Herring, Joseph T.		01/00
CPT	Becker, I.		17/00
CPT	Downey, J. W.		16/00
CPT	Tripp, E. R.		03/00
CPT	Page, C. R.		16/00
1LT	Geraci, Joseph T.		03/00
LTC	McClean, Charles B.	Regimental Executive Officer.	25/00
SGM	Wood, J. H.	Battalion Sergeant Major.	02/00
SGM	Smith, Stuart	Battalion Sergeant Major.	02/00
SGM	Alvey, H. C.	Regimental Sergeant Major.	03/00
1SG	Holliday, Henry, Jr.		03/00
1SG	Haines, W. J.		03/00
SGT	Casey, James C.	Chief Musician.	03/00
	Jewell, H. J.	Color Sergeant.	02/00
	Holidayoke, D. F.	Color Sergeant.	03/00
	Bray, Edmund H.	Hospital Steward.	01/00
	Kneisley, Herbert L.	Hospital Steward. Listed on B CO payroll 16-20 FEB.	01/00
	Lamb, C. G.	Hospital Steward.	03/00

Company A, Cumberland

CPT	Ullrich, Harry	Company Commander.	06/08
1LT	Schley, Harry J.	Company Executive Officer. Total service not listed.	
1SG	Farmer, James G.	Company First Sergeant. Total service not listed.	
SGT	Buckey, William	Total service not listed.	
SGT	Weber, Harvey E. (C.)	Quartermaster Sergeant. Total service not listed.	
CPL	White, James G.	Total service not listed.	
CPL	Ritchey, William M.	Total service not listed.	
CPL	Magruder, Edward K.	Total service not listed.	
CPL	Smith, Louis A.	Total service not listed.	
CPL	Dorris, John B. W.	Total service not listed.	
PVT	Messenger, John R.	Total service not listed.	
PVT	McAllister, Joseph V.	Total service not listed.	
PVT	Kennedy, Harry	Total service not listed.	
PVT	McLaughlin, George B.	Total service not listed.	
PVT	Shipe, Charles A.	Total service not listed.	
PVT	Ruppert, Frank	Total service not listed.	
PVT	Brenaman, H. L.	Total service not listed.	
PVT	Porter, H. Morton	Total service not listed.	
PVT	Preston, William L.	Total service not listed.	
PVT	Baylor, Robert M.	Total service not listed.	
PVT	O'Hara, Charles	Total service not listed.	
PVT	O'Neill, John M.	Total service not listed.	
PVT	Metz, Robert W.	Total service not listed.	
PVT	Hally, Albert L.	Total service not listed.	
PVT	Pelton, James	Total service not listed.	
PVT	Preston, Claude	Total service not listed.	
PVT	Carpenter, C. S.	Total service not listed.	
PVT	Enos, C. O.	Total service not listed.	
PVT	Graham, Charles E.	Total service not listed.	
PVT	Feaga, H. C.	Total service not listed.	
PVT	Dixon, A. P.	Total service not listed.	
PVT	Dawes, Joseph B.	Total service not listed.	
PVT	Clark, Thomas A.	Total service not listed.	

Company B, Hagerstown

CPT	Fisher, George L.	Company Commander.	23/00
1LT	Sands, William E.	Company Executive Officer.	19/00
2LT	Tynenson (Tynerson), Arthur A.		05/10
1SG	Small, Ruben K.	Company First Sergeant.	05/09
SGT	Bowers, Charles H.		05/00
SGT	Sharar, Walter		05/00
SGT	Cottrill, Leo D.		05/09
CPL	Hager, Richard		02/08
CPL	Alsip, Charles M.		02/07
CPL	Gossard, Martin L.		04/00
CPL	Barber, Joseph H.		05/00
CPL	Lamar, Marion (Bruce)		02/09
PVT	Grove, Melchor C.		00/09
PVT	Knode, Alfred		00/10
PVT	Kretzer, Henry		00/09
PVT	Frush (Fresh), Walter H.		00/08
PVT	Davies, Rowland J.		02/00
PVT	Favorite, Edward T.		04/00
PVT	Barncord, Jerry		01/00
PVT	Davies, John H.		05/00
PVT	Bryan, James W.		00/10
PVT	Zinkand, John S.	Enlisted 19 JAN 1904.	00/01
PVT	Tall, Lewis C.		01/00
PVT	Jones, Albert		00/08
PVT	Shirley, John D.		02/07
PVT	Jones, Lewis M.		01/02
PVT	Rowe, Robert B.		01/06
PVT	Hilton, William B.	Enlisted 8 FEB 1904.	00/00
PVT	Moore, Alex N.		02/03
PVT	Trone, Franklin A.		02/03
PVT	Sprecher, Emory R.		02/00
PVT	Morgan, Hugh B.		02/00
PVT	Baker, Albert		02/00

PVT	Hose, John S.		02/00
PVT	Good, Herbert J.		02/00
PVT	Fisher, James Ray (Roy)		02/00
PVT	Forsyth, Christ		00/03
PVT	Baker, Oliver L.		02/00

Company C, Cambridge

CPT	Latimer, Thomas E.	Company Commander.	01/03
1LT	Hurst, J. Howard	Company Executive Officer.	01/03
2LT	Tschautre (Tschantre), Leon E.	Listed on L CO payroll 16-18 FEB.	01/03
1SG	Trice, V. Calvin	First Sergeant, C CO. Listed on L CO payroll 16-18 FEB.	01/03
SGT	Collins, James Thomas	Listed on L CO payroll 16-18 FEB.	01/03
SGT	Wirz, Ernest		01/03
SGT	Singer, Max	Listed on L CO payroll 16-18 FEB.	01/03
CPL	Jones, J. Radcliffe, Jr.	Listed on L CO payroll 16-18 FEB.	01/03
CPL	Barkley, Jesse	Listed on L CO payroll 16-18 FEB.	01/03
CPL	Hoge, William F.		01/03
CPL	Waller, William		01/03
PVT	Hirt, Adolph	Listed on L CO payroll 16-18 FEB.	01/03
PVT	Latham, Clarence		01/03
PVT	Mowbray, William	Listed on L CO payroll 16-18 FEB.	01/03
PVT	Clark, William H.	Listed on L CO payroll 16-18 FEB.	01/03
PVT	Clark, George		01/03
PVT	Butler, James		01/03
PVT	Anderson, James	Company Cook. Total enlistment not listed.	
PVT	Wherrett, Harry		01/03
PVT	Wilson, Edward	Listed on L CO payroll 16-18 FEB.	01/03
PVT	Wright, Lyle	Listed on L CO payroll 16-18 FEB.	01/03
PVT	Wallace, Allen	Listed on L CO payroll 16-18 FEB.	01/03
PVT	Vane, Roy C. (Leroy)	Listed on L CO payroll 16-18 FEB.	01/03
PVT	Reese, Howard	Listed on L CO payroll 16-18 FEB.	01/03
PVT	Percy, E.		01/03
PVT	Parker, Clarence	Listed on L CO payroll 16-18 FEB.	01/03
PVT	Tucker, N. C.		01/03
PVT	Andrews, Roland		01/03

PVT	Manner, William	Listed on L CO payroll 16-18 FEB.	01/03
PVT	Willey, Frank	Signed with an "X." Listed on L CO payroll 16-18 FEB.	01/03
PVT	Hoge, Otto H.	Listed on L CO payroll 16-18 FEB.	01/03
PVT	Adams, Sebastion H.	Listed on L CO payroll 16-18 FEB.	01/03
PVT	Henry, Harry E.	Listed on L CO payroll 16-18 FEB.	01/03
PVT	Brannock, Charles	Listed on L CO payroll 16-18 FEB.	01/03
PVT	Hassett, T. H. (Howard)	Listed on L CO payroll 16-18 FEB.	01/03
PVT	Dunn, W.		01/03
PVT	Dunn, Richard	Listed on L CO payroll 16-18 FEB.	01/03
PVT	Goslyn, Charles (Charley)	Listed on L CO payroll 16-18 FEB.	01/03
PVT	Airey, Ernest	Listed on L CO payroll 16-18 FEB.	01/03
PVT	Malone, T. Henry	Listed on L CO payroll 16-18 FEB.	01/03
PVT	Parks, Lawson	Listed on L CO payroll 16-18 FEB.	01/03
PVT	Foble, John B.	Company Musician.	01/03
PVT	Merrick, Wilson G.		01/03
PVT	Colbourn (Calbourn), George		01/03

Company D, Bel Air

CPT	Reckord, Milton A.	Company Commander.	03/00
1LT	Rosner, Sterling D.	Company Executive Officer.	06/00
2LT	Smith, Silas B.		09/00
SGT	Keen, Walter K.		03/00
SGT	McComas, Walter R.		03/01
SGT	Colder, Albert F.		08/00
SGT	Rouston, William A.		03/00
CPL	Colder, E. Hall		06/00
CPL	Spencer, Cecil C.		03/03
CPL	Brounel, J. Wallace		02/08
CPL	Carroll, James R.		08/00
PVT	Hanna, James C.		02/05
PVT	Kisling, Norman L.		00/01
PVT	George, John		02/00
PVT	Tucker, Laurence		00/01
PVT	Kisling, Willie S.		00/01
PVT	Dean, James N.		02/11

PVT	Starr, Asel	02/10
PVT	Harward, J. Wilson	02/03
PVT	Flowers, Harry	02/00
PVT	Flowers, Warren	02/01
PVT	Archer, J. Glasgow	02/10
PVT	Hopkins, T. Kenton	02/10
PVT	Whiteford, Frank	00/09
PVT	Knofler, Melvin C.	02/11
PVT	Milley (Milnay), Jacob H.	02/11
PVT	Waters, H. Burton	03/03
PVT	Watkins, Burton	00/01
PVT	Archer, R. Harris, Jr.	02/11
PVT	Reynolds, Frank M.	02/10
PVT	Hollingsworth, D. F. (Richard)	02/07
PVT	Wildason, John	00/08
PVT	Watson, James O.	02/07
PVT	Norris, James F.	00/08
PVT	Doggett, William H.	00/09
PVT	Shertzer, Harry A.	08/00
PVT	Favour, John G.	02/07
PVT	Girvin, John N.	02/10
PVT	Warnick, John	02/09
PVT	Hall, Thomas W.	03/09
PVT	Trago, Harris	02/10
PVT	Preston, Reynolds	00/01
PVT	Streett, Alex D.	02/10
PVT	Scholpp, Charles	02/00
PVT	Colder, George C.	00/08
PVT	DeBon, Leon	00/08
PVT	Butler, William P.	02/11
PVT	Baker, Alonzo P.	02/03

Company E, Elkton

1LT	Morgan, John A.	Company Commander. Commissioned 14 APR 1902.	10/11
2LT	Constable, William P.	Company Executive Officer. Commissioned 7 AUG 1902. Total service not listed.	
1SG	Lewis, Herbert	Company First Sergeant.	03/11
SGT	Reeder, Clinton		03/09
SGT	Kelly, John (T.)		03/09
SGT	Johnson, Alan D.		01/06
SGT	Ash, Joshua M.	Quartermaster Sergeant.	12/00
CPL	Hitchner, J. Gorman		07/11
CPL	Finnan, Cletus		02/10
CPL	Mahoney, William J.		02/11
CPL	Reeder, Harvey		03/10
CPL	McCauley, J. Hayes		02/07
CPL	Wright, George		03/09
PVT	Racine, Harry		03/07
PVT	Ross, Joseph W.		02/06
PVT	Mahoney, J. Thomas		02/11
PVT	Vesper, John	Enlisted 26 JAN 1904.	
PVT	McDonald, James		00/08
PVT	Clark, Isaac N.		07/06
PVT	MacNeal, Fred R.		01/00
PVT	Corridean, Joseph		00/09
PVT	Potts, Oscar		00/11
PVT	Foreacre, George G.		00/09
PVT	Holmes, Charles F.		02/11
PVT	Hitchner, John G.	Enlisted 8 FEB 1904.	
PVT	Lang, William		01/07
PVT	Ayers, Charles H., Jr.		01/03
PVT	Clark, Robert S.		13/03
PVT	Daniels, Charles S. (L.)		02/10
PVT	Wright, William T.		00/09
PVT	Mahoney, Harry E.		02/10
PVT	Cameron, Andrew		00/10
PVT	Rutter, George W.		00/11

PVT	Simpers, Edgar T.		01/08
PVT	Scott, Frank		00/09
PVT	Sterling, Frank P.		01/07
PVT	Thompson, George A.		03/11
	Jones, Edward W.	Company Musician.	00/11
	Morgan, John A.	Company Musician.	00/11

Company F, Easton

CPT	Adams, Charles W.	Company Commander.	01.08
1LT	Lednum, Jesse A.	Company Executive Officer.	01/08
2LT	Turner, Henry P.		01/08
1SG	Summers, Clarence A.	Company First Sergeant.	01/08
SGT	Soulsby, C. M. T.	Quartermaster Sergeant.	01/08
CPL	Hardcastle, Robert		01/08
CPL	Whitman, Walter W.		01/08
CPL	Grace, Philip G.	Listed on L CO payroll 16-18 FEB.	01/08
CPL	Hammond, Charles P.	Listed on L CO payroll 16-18 FEB.	01/08
CPL	Page, William E.	Listed on L CO payroll 16-18 FEB.	01/08
PVT	Dooling, Percy	Listed on L CO payroll 16-18 FEB.	01/06
PVT	Wood, Walter B.		01/08
PVT	Loveday, William N.	Listed on L CO payroll 16-18 FEB.	01/02
PVT	Merrick, Charles A.	Listed on L CO payroll 16-18 FEB.	01/01
PVT	Ball, Joseph	Listed on L CO payroll 16-18 FEB. Arrested with PVT George Parrott for profanity arising from altercation in front of the city hall, Ball was jailed for carrying a concealed weapon (iron knuckles). He paid a fine and was released four days later.	00/08
PVT	Page, Milton	Listed on L CO payroll 16-18 FEB.	01/06
PVT	Collison, William		01/00
PVT	Parrott, George W.	Total service not listed. On 16 FEB, Parrott was involved in an altercation with civilians in front of the city hall and arrested with PVT Joseph Ball for profanity. He was released after paying a small fine. Ball was jailed.	
PVT	Doyle, Samuel M.		00/09
PVT	Patterson, William	Total service not listed. Listed on L CO payroll 16-18 FEB.	
PVT	Ferguson, William A.		01/00
PVT	Smith, Cleveland S.	Listed on L CO payroll 16-18 FEB.	01/08
PVT	Greenhawk, Frank A.	Listed on L CO payroll 16-18 FEB.	00/09

PVT	Smith, Arthur J.	Listed on L CO payroll 16-18 FEB.	00/09
PVT	Sparklin(g), Fredrick	Listed on L CO payroll 16-18 FEB.	01/08
PVT	Tarbutton, Charles M.	Enlisted 8 FEB 1904. Listed on L CO payroll 16-18 FEB.	00/00
PVT	Yewell, Walter H.		01/06
PVT	Ferguson, Thomas	Enlisted 8 FEB 1904. Listed on L CO payroll 16-18 FEB.	00/00
PVT	Love, Harry		00/08
PVT	Collison, John W.		01/08
PVT	Eason, Norman A.		01/08
PVT	Tarbutton, Olin	Enlisted 8 FEB 1904.	00/00
PVT	Bowers, Howell B.	Listed on L CO payroll 16-18 FEB.	01/08
PVT	Wallace, Robert B.	Listed on L CO payroll 16-18 FEB.	00/09
PVT	Warrington, William E.		01/06
	Weston, Harry J.	Company Musician.	01/06
	Collison, Walter T.	Company Musician.	01/08

Company G, Annapolis

CPT	Porter, Phil E.	Company Commander.	17/10
1LT	Tydings, George R.	Company Executive Officer.	17/10
2LT	Tydings, George T.	Listed on M CO payroll 16-20 FEB.	09/06
SGT	Mitchell, Phil E.		07/00
SGT	Freeman, Joseph P.		09/07
SGT	Beall, James H. V.		03/11
SGT	Sweet, Charles A.		06/04
SGT	Geraci, Frank B.	Quartermaster Sergeant.	09/07
CPL	Jones, Edward J.		02/11
CPL	Koch, John S.		06/11
CPL	Gardiner, George A.		03/00
CPL	Hopkins, Edgar E.		03/01
CPL	Cox, Joseph Harry	Listed on M CO payroll 16-20 FEB.	01/06
PVT	Campbell, William E.	Listed on M CO payroll 16-20 FEB.	00/10
PVT	Carroll, Wallace	Listed on M CO payroll 16-20 FEB.	00/06
PVT	Chappell, John E.	Enlisted 8 FEB 1904.	00/00
PVT	Cole, John Herbert	Listed on M CO payroll 16-20 FEB.	00/09
PVT	Collins, Charles		09/00
PVT	Sands, Thomas E.		00/06

Rank	Name	Notes	Service
PVT	Collins, John P.		00/11
PVT	Thompson, Charles		01/09
PVT	Crosby, Thomas J.		03/00
PVT	Tull, James	Listed on M CO payroll 16-20 FEB.	01/04
PVT	Fisher, John H.	Listed on M CO payroll 16-20 FEB.	03/03
PVT	Myers (Meyers), David V.	Musician. Listed on M CO payroll 16-20 FEB.	01/06
PVT	Miller, Theodore	Enlisted 8 FEB 1904. Miller was "thrown from the top of a trolley pole on Pratt St" while working with the Signal Corps. He suffered only a bruised heel.	
PVT	Hyde, Benjamin	Paid $1.10/day 7-15 FEB and paid $1.00/day 16-20 FEB. Listed on M CO payroll 16-20 FEB.	03/10
PVT	Mayo, George B.		02/07
PVT	Ivey, James		01/03
PVT	Mitchell, William A.	Listed on M CO payroll 16-20 FEB.	01/09
PVT	Lowman, John R.		03/10
PVT	Nelson, Benjamin		00/03
PVT	Meade, William A.		03/00
PVT	Hyde, Daniel	Listed on M CO payroll 16-20 FEB.	00/08
PVT	Jacobs, Arthur G.	Paid $1.00/day 7-15 FEB and paid $1.10/day 16-20 FEB. Listed on M CO payroll 16-20 FEB.	01/06
PVT	McCann, John H.		01/06
PVT	Hubbard, William	Listed on M CO payroll 16-20 FEB.	03/11
PVT	Parkinson, Joseph	Listed on M CO payroll 16-20 FEB.	01/06
PVT	Pennell, Hazen	Listed on M CO payroll 16-20 FEB.	03/00
PVT	Carroll, Charles W.	Enlisted 29 JAN 1904. Listed on M CO payroll 16-20 FEB.	00/00
PVT	Denver, W. Frank	Enlisted 8 FEB 1904.	00/00
PVT	Holland, Fred	Listed on M CO payroll 16-20 FEB.	01/02

Company H, Westminster

Rank	Name	Notes
2LT	Smith, Claude Tilden	Company Commander, H CO. Listed on B CO payroll 16-20 FEB. Total service not listed. Current commission 8 JAN 1901.
1SG	Weigh, John N.	Company First Sergeant. Total service not listed.
SGT	Holton, Charles A.	Total service not listed.
SGT	Lawyer, William G. (Grove)	Total service not listed. Listed on B CO payroll 16-20 FEB.

SGT	Barnes, Charles F.	Total service not listed. Listed on B CO payroll 16-20 FEB.
SGT	Shriver, Edward S.	Total service not listed.
CPL	Hann, John R.	Total service not listed. Listed on B CO payroll 16-20 FEB.
CPL	Frizzell, William E.	Total service not listed. Paid $1.25/day as a CPL 7-15 FEB, paid $1.00/day as a PVT 16-20 FEB. Listed on B CO payroll 16-20 FEB.
CPL	Weeks, William W.	Total service not listed.
CPL	Holmes, Presley H.	Total service not listed. Paid $1.25/day as a CPL 7-15 FEB and paid $1.00/day as a PVT 16-20 FEB. Listed on B CO payroll 16-20 FEB.
CPL	Dell, Winter C.	Total service not listed. Paid $1.25/day as a CPL 7-15 FEB, paid $1.00/day as a PVT 16-20 FEB. Listed on B CO payroll 16-20 FEB.
PVT	Agnew, William J.	Total service not listed. Listed on B CO payroll 16-20 FEB.
PVT	Arnold, Lyman M.	Total service not listed.
PVT	Barnes, Clarence	Total service not listed. Listed on B CO payroll 16-20 FEB.
PVT	Barnes, Howard J.	Total service not listed. Listed on B CO payroll 16-20 FEB.
PVT	Bentz, Joseph W.	Total service not listed.
PVT	Bitzel, Philip W.	Total service not listed.
PVT	Bollinger, Scott C.	Total service not listed.
PVT	Engleman, David J.	Total service not listed. Listed on B CO payroll 16-20 FEB.
PVT	Stone, William J.	Total service not listed. Listed on B CO payroll 16-20 FEB.
PVT	Thomson, James H.	Total service not listed.
PVT	Crumberker (Crumbacker), Arthur	Total service not listed.
PVT	Van Fassen, Irvin J.	Total service not listed.
PVT	Durben, Roy John	Total service not listed. Listed on B CO payroll 16-20 FEB.
PVT	Van Fassen, Dudley H.	Total service not listed. Listed on B CO payroll 16-20 FEB.
PVT	Eisenhart, John W.	Total service not listed.
PVT	Webster, Elisha B.	Total service not listed.
PVT	Erb, Carl	Total service not listed.
PVT	Zendgraft, Joseph F. (T.)	Total service not listed.

PVT	Fowler, Charles F. (T.)	Total service not listed. Listed on B CO payroll 16-20 FEB.	
PVT	Zendgraft, William D.	Total service not listed. Listed on B CO payroll 16-20 FEB.	
PVT	Grimes, William Taylor	Total service not listed. Listed on B CO payroll 16-20 FEB.	
PVT	Brown, Edward H.	Total service not listed. Listed on B CO payroll 16-20 FEB.	
PVT	Leister, Guy W.	Total service not listed. Listed on B CO payroll 16-20 FEB.	
PVT	Dell, Russell F.	Total service not listed. Listed on B CO payroll 16-20 FEB.	
PVT	Manger, Faryl C. (Joseph)	Total service not listed. Listed on B CO payroll 16-20 FEB.	
PVT	Roberts, Charles S.	Total service not listed.	
PVT	Simonson, H. A.	Total service not listed.	
PVT	Leffert, William E.	Total service not listed. Listed on B CO payroll 16-20 FEB.	
PVT	Manning, John P.	Total service not listed. Listed on B CO payroll 16-20 FEB.	
PVT	Eckenrode, Joseph G.	Total service not listed. Listed on B CO payroll 16-20 FEB.	
PVT	Englar, Frank, Jr.	Total service not listed. Listed on B CO payroll 16-20 FEB.	
PVT	Fisher, Charles E.	Total service not listed. Listed on B CO payroll 16-20 FEB.	
PVT	Fowler, John D.	Total service not listed.	
PVT	Heird, Howell H.	Total service not listed. Listed on B CO payroll 16-20 FEB.	

Company I, Salisbury

CPT	Caulbourn, L. P.	Company Commander.	02/10
2LT	Owens, H. Winter	Company Executive Officer.	02/10
1SG	Douglass, Samuel R.	Company First Sergeant.	02/10
SGT	Chatham, James S.		02/10
SGT	Turner, Benjamin W.		02/10
SGT	Grier, Fred A., Jr.		02/10
SGT	Brown, John W.		02/10
CPL	Flemming, Archibald J.		02/07
CPL	Hayman, Sewell P.		02/08
CPL	Hillman, E. W.		02/10
CPL	Disharoon, Lein (Levin)		02/10

CPL	Gillis, C. Lee		02/05
PVT	Adkins, Charles E.		00/10
PVT	Adkins, Joda		00/07
PVT	Bennett, Charles E.		02/10
PVT	White, W. W.		00/02
PVT	Humphreys, Louis		02/09
PVT	Bozman, James		02/10
PVT	Humphreys, G. R.		02/10
PVT	Downing, Cannon J.		02/10
PVT	Johnson, J. Roy		00/07
PVT	Farlow, Harvey G.		02/10
PVT	Livingston, J. R. P., Jr.		02/09
PVT	Holt, E. W.		02/09
PVT	Mitchell, P. R.	Signed with an "X."	01/06
PVT	Hudson, John	Signed with an "X."	00/07
PVT	Farlow, Charles		02/10
PVT	Hammond, Hiram P.		02/10
PVT	Holt, S. E.		02/10
PVT	Collins, John L.		02/08
PVT	Moore, William	Signed with an "X."	02/10
PVT	Ruark, S. L.		01/07
PVT	Smith, C. W.		02/10
PVT	Sturgis, H. W.		00/07
PVT	Brewington, W. K.		02/09

Company K, Rockville

CPT	Talbot, Thomas M.	Company Commander.	01/03
1LT	Reading, W. M.	Company Executive Officer.	01/03
2LT	Brewer, William R.		01/03
SGT	Carr, William B.		01/03
SGT	Kelchner, G. A. M.		01/03
SGT	Pass, William		01/03
SGT	Ricketts, C.		01/03
CPL	Brewer, Nicholas		01/03
CPL	Moulden, Harry		01/03
CPL	Hilton, John E.		01/03
CPL	Smith, Roy E.		01/03

CPL	Whipp, Arthur		01/03
CPL	Glascott, H. C.		01/03
CPL	Collins, John		01/03
PVT	Allnutt, George B.		01/03
PVT	Benson, T. B.		01/03
PVT	Beard, Spencer		01/03
PVT	Brewer, Lloyd		01/03
PVT	Carr, H. S.		01/03
PVT	Carr, D. J.		01/03
PVT	Connelly, S. B.		01/03
PVT	West, Joe		01/03
PVT	Kuts (Keets), Edward		02/08
PVT	Packard, Joseph		01/03
PVT	Rabbitt, Harvey	Returned to Montgomery County to be with sister who was suffering from pneumonia.	01/03
PVT	Greene, Allie		01/03
PVT	Rabbitt, Charles		01/03
PVT	Higgins, J. J., Jr.		01/03
PVT	Ricketts, R. J.		01/03
PVT	Mills, N.		01/03
PVT	Ricketts, Preston		01/03
PVT	Offutt, William W.		00/05
PVT	Riggs, Douglass		01/03
PVT	Day, Edward		01/03
PVT	Mills, A.		01/03
PVT	McCollough, Edward		01/03
PVT	Poss, C. J.		01/03
PVT	Herbert, Orril		01/03
PVT	Trail, Carlton		01/03
PVT	Trammell, Joseph E.		01/03
PVT	Waters, Clark		00/02
PVT	Emrich, George		01/03
PVT	Fish, R. S.		01/03

Company L, Centreville

CPT	Wilson, John E.	Company Commander.	02/11
1LT	Parvis, Joseph M.	Company Executive Officer. Total service not listed.	
2LT	Middleton, James H.		02/11
1SG	Hayden, Alfred C.	Company First Sergeant.	02/11
SGT	Davis, Thomas H.		02/11
SGT	Davis, Claude G.		02/11
SGT	Hayden, Edward G.		02/11
SGT	Warren, Herbert H.	Paid $1.25/day as a CPL 7-15 FEB, paid $1.50/day as a SGT 16-18 FEB.	02/11
CPL	Roberts, James L.		02/11
PVT	Bailey, William C.		02/11
PVT	Councill, Frank		01/02
PVT	Councill (Council), Willie	Signed with an "X."	01/08
PVT	Faulkner, James O.		01/10
PVT	Flowers, Holton H.		02/11
PVT	Goldsborough, James P.		01/10
PVT	Hayden, Lloyd T.		02/11
PVT	Holden, James H.		02/11
PVT	Howser, Charles H. (Harry)		01/10
PVT	Chance, Willie Julian		02/11
PVT	Jester, Washington		00/09
PVT	Turner, Ray	Musician.	02/11
PVT	Kirby, Thomas		02/11
PVT	Vasey, Horace		02/11
PVT	Meredith, Alfred C.		02/11
PVT	Woolford, Henry C.		02/11
PVT	Morgan, James		02/11
PVT	Bryan, Raymond C.		01/01
PVT	Roe, J. Wesley	Listed on L CO payroll 16-18 FEB.	01/01
PVT	Sparks, William S.		02/11
PVT	Lane, Thomas Roy		01/06
PVT	Meredith, Luther H.		02/11
PVT	Pardee, John S. E.		01/10
PVT	Rothwell, Edward K.		00/09

Company M, Annapolis

CPT	Riley, Hugh R.	Company Commander.	02/10
1LT	Holidayoke, William E.	Company Executive Officer.	05/10
2LT	Crauford (Cranford), Zachariah S.		02/10
1SG	Beall, William V.	First Sergeant. Paid $1.75/day 7-15 FEB, paid $1.93/day 16-20 FEB.	05/10
SGT	Chinn, E. Lacy	Quartermaster Sergeant.	02/10
SGT	Johnson, Harry M.		02/10
SGT	Pennell, Joseph R.		02/10
SGT	Beall, Harry L.		02/10
SGT	Gates, John L.		02/10
CPL	Myers, Charles E.		02/10
CPL	Myers, Louis B.		02/06
CPL	Le Tournan, Harry		02/10
CPL	Taylor, John N.		02/10
CPL	Strohm, John C.		02/10
CPL	Howard, Harvey		02/10
PVT	Ayers, Warren C.		01/00
PVT	Bean, Harry E.		02/00
PVT	Brackett, James F. (Frank)		02/00
PVT	Brown, Howard		02/00
PVT	Bourke, Benjamin F.		00/06
PVT	Boush, James C.		02/10
PVT	Cox, Harry E.		02/10
PVT	Vanous, William J.		02/00
PVT	Ward, William H.		02/00
PVT	Wood, Ernest P.		01/00
PVT	Gunther, Chriss		01/02
PVT	Sears, Cheston B.		01/00
PVT	Cornell, Eugene M.		02/00
PVT	Sears, George W.	During the fire service, Sears and a W. Oberry worked as assistant cooks under the direction of chief cook Benjamin F. Burke.	02/00
PVT	Davis, Daniel		02/00
PVT	Sears, Samuel J.		01/00
PVT	Ebling, William		01/00

PVT	Smith, George W.	02/00
PVT	Howard, Oliver E.	01/00
PVT	Small, Joseph T.	01/00
PVT	Kelley, John H.	02/00
PVT	Taylor, Charles N.	02/00
PVT	League, Eugene O.	01/00
PVT	Taylor, Frank B.	02/00
PVT	Marshall, Horace	01/00
PVT	Thomas, William E.	02/00
PVT	Nichols, Thomas D.	02/00
PVT	Gaither, Bernard	02/00
PVT	Rulhnan (Rullman), William	01/00
PVT	Cranford, Ralph R.	02/00
PVT	Davey, Raymond O. J.	02/00
PVT	Obery, Charles H.	02/10
PVT	Hinton, George L.	02/00
PVT	Klakring, Leslie	02/00
PVT	Mace, Jesse	02/00
PVT	Mitchell, George W.	02/00
PVT	Obery, William J.	02/10

Fourth Regiment, Infantry

Field and Staff

COL	Howard, Willard	Regimental Commander.	15/06
MAJ	Pennington, D. F.	Regimental Quartermaster.	18/00
MAJ	Robinson, George T.	Son of MAJ George T. Robinson, Sr. (US Army), engineer and cartographer responsible for a "noteworthy" map of the west in the collection of the Newberry Library, Chicago, Illinois.	13/03
MAJ	Jones, Harry C.		06/06
MAJ	Ullrich, S. S.	Surgeon.	07/10
CPT	Burck, William A.		12/10
CPT	Hill, Charles Irving	Assistant Surgeon.	03/07
CPT	Sayler, J. A.		03/00
CPT	Uhler (Uhlen), W. D.	Regimental Provost Marshall.	04/00
CPT	MacCalman, Duncan	Assistant Surgeon.	06/00

CPT	Townsend, W. Guy	Assistant Surgeon.	03/07
CPT	Kingsbury, L. L.	Regimental Commissary Officer.	06/08
LT	Wischmeyer, Ed, Jr.	Battalion Adjutant.	02/11
LTC	Supplee, J. Frank	Regimental Executive Officer.	13/00
LT	Ryley, J. Frank	Probably an Adjutant.	18/00
LT	Hahn, Charles	Battalion Adjutant.	15/00
SGM	Watts, C. R.	Regimental Sergeant Major.	00/01
SGM	Loomis, Charles L.	Battalion Sergeant Major.	09/03
SGM	Meyers, George J.	Battalion Sergeant Major.	10/04
SGT	Brown, William B.	Commissary Sergeant.	00/08
SGT	Renehan, W.	Quartermaster Sergeant.	06/11
SGT	Thomas, Clark	Ordnance Sergeant.	14/08
SGT	Loane, J. D.	Color Sergeant.	05/10
	Rice, L. G.		15/09
	Krauss, S.	Chief Musician.	16/10
	Binau, A.	Hospital steward.	01/08
	Bell, C. K.	Regimental Chaplain.	01/05
	Burke, E.	Hospital steward.	01/05
	Hickman, C. D.	Hospital steward.	02/10
	Wooden, H. E.	Hospital steward.	00/11
	Hartman, H. M.	Hospital steward.	00/09

Headquarters Company

1SG	Taylor, W. R.	First Sergeant.	07/00
SGT	Derreth, J.		03/08
SGT	Eck, Charles		03/10
SGT	Bitz, F.		00/11
PVT	Walters, Morris		00/09
PVT	Allerton, S. M.		01/04
PVT	Blank, L. N.		01/08
PVT	Bell, G. W.		01/03
PVT	Bucklen, E. R.		01/03
PVT	Bagon, W. J.		01/04
PVT	Daumman, H. S.		00/03
PVT	Neary, A. G.		00/08
PVT	Goudy, N. A.		00/04
PVT	Perkins, J. A.		00/03

PVT	Gould, D. U.	01/03
PVT	Pfluger, C. J.	01/03
PVT	Kessler, C.	01/04
PVT	Rivialles, F. T.	01/03
PVT	Long, W. T.	01/04
PVT	Gardner, H. K.	03/10
PVT	Geist, Walter S.	00/10
PVT	Lyons, J. W.	00/10
PVT	Linson, K. L.	01/04
PVT	Roberts, C. H.	00/09
PVT	Rosenstock, G. E.	00/08
PVT	Swain, R. C.	00/11
PVT	Wiggins, T. B.	01/04
PVT	Wiggin, D. C.	01/03
PVT	Rayne, J. E.	01/04
PVT	Summerbell, Ferris	01/04
PVT	Burness, J. M.	00/08
PVT	McComas, J. L.	00/10
PVT	Garrett, William T.	00/01
PVT	Jones, A. B.	01/03
CIV	Lewis, R. W.	
CIV	Robinson, William	
CIV	Krauss, Perry	
CIV	Wooden, William T.	
CIV	Hamilton, S.	
CIV	Johns, W. J.	
CIV	McKenna, William J.	
CIV	Tyler, Douglas	
CIV	Hammond, James Edward	
CIV	Passley, T.	
CIV	Dennis, H.	
CIV	Shenley (Shancley), James	
CIV	Beale, S. J.	
CIV	Beach, Charles	
CIV	Trogood, Charles	

CIV	Williams, A. (Addine)		
CIV	Lee, Clarence		
CIV	Bond, Oliver		
CIV	Miller, E.		
CIV	Tinson, Clarence		
CIV	Smith, Ed. F.		
CIV	Thomas, J. E.		
CIV	Wooden, S.		
CIV	Griffin, B.		
CIV	Brown, Richard	Signed with an "X."	
CIV	Bond, A.		
CIV	Davis, Charles	Signed with an "X."	
CIV	Dorsey, William		

Company A

1LT	Rittenhouse, D. M.	Company Commander, A CO. Listed on H CO payroll 16-22 FEB.	01/00
2LT	Buffington, A. G.	Company Executive Officer. Listed on D CO payroll 16-22 FEB.	01/00
QM	Swain, Charles P.	Quartermaster Sergeant.	08/07
1SG	Burns, Edward J.	First Sergeant.	12/03
SGT	Lewis, D. C.		12/03
SGT	Kraskell, J. H.		12/03
SGT	Hodeck, Joseph		06/04
SGT	Beale, James		05/00
CPL	Crooks, J. Irvin	Paid $1.38/day 7-15 FEB. Listed on M CO payroll and paid $1.25/day, 16-23 FEB.	05/11
CPL	Jones, A. W.		06/00
CPL	Taylor, G. W.		04/09
CPL	Times, Alex		07/03
PVT	Haupt, James H.		00/10
PVT	Hildebrandt, Charles H.	Listed on D CO payroll 16-22 FEB.	00/11
PVT	Thomas, J. Edward		00/10
PVT	Kurt, William		02/09
PVT	Shields, William C.		00/10
PVT	Smith, George	Listed on L CO payroll 16-23 FEB.	00/08
PVT	Beall, Benjamin Lloyd		00/11
PVT	Mace, Laurence	Listed on L CO payroll 16-23 FEB.	00/03

PVT	Allen, Thomas		00/09
PVT	Reynolds, George	Listed on L CO payroll 16-23 FEB.	00/02
PVT	Weise, Edward	Paid $1.00/day 7-15 FEB, paid $1.10/day 16-22 FEB.	03/00
PVT	Poole, W. H.	Listed on L CO payroll 16-23 FEB.	00/08
PVT	Gaylord (Gayland), J. Clinton	Listed on L CO payroll 16-23 FEB.	01/03
PVT	Carroll, Joseph	Listed on D CO payroll 16-22 FEB.	00/08
PVT	Reiner, Jacob		03/00
PVT	Moore, Charles		01/01
PVT	Meyers, Edward	Listed on K CO payroll 16-20 FEB as "In City Jail." Meyers was arrested with PVT Harry Embe and George Russell, a civilian, for stealing a fire extinguisher. All were jailed but the state declined prosecution in March.	02/10
PVT	Brent, John P.	Listed on D CO payroll 16-22 FEB.	00/08
PVT	Ackerman, John	Listed on D CO payroll 16-22 FEB.	02/01
PVT	Haukin, William	Listed on D CO payroll 16-22 FEB.	00/08
PVT	Burton, Clifton	Listed on D CO payroll 16-22 FEB.	00/01
PVT	Clathey, James M.	Listed on L CO payroll 16-23 FEB.	00/10
PVT	Donnelly, F. B.	Listed on L CO payroll 16-23 FEB.	00/10
PVT	Morrison, T. E.		01/03
PVT	Glanding, W. L.		00/10
PVT	Weems, F. S.	Listed on D CO payroll 16-22 FEB.	00/03
PVT	Dodson, Harry	Listed on L CO payroll 16-23 FEB.	00/08
PVT	Shipley, C. R.	Listed on L CO payroll 16-23 FEB.	00/08
PVT	Peters, Andrew (Andy)		00/08
PVT	Mullin, P.		00/08
PVT	Moore, Herman	Enlisted 23 JUN 1903. Listed on E CO payroll 16-22 FEB.	00/08

Company B

CPT	Haupt, G. F.	Company Commander.	18/06
1LT	Jones, N. L.	Total service not listed.	00/00
2LT	Lyon, C. L.	Company Executive Officer.	13/00
1SG	Binnix, C. W.	First Sergeant.	15/10
SGT	Rine, G. D.		07/02
SGT	Firsch, H. E.		10/02
SGT	Murrill, C. E.		07/07

SGT	Willis, E. S.		06/11
SGT	Simon, J.	Current enlistment began 12 APR 1901.	00/00
CPL	Winslow, N.		05/10
CPL	McCarthy, W. J.		02/11
CPL	Monthly, E.		05/10
CPL	Fisher, H. E.		05/08
CPL	Phelan, N.		02/11
CPL	Ratcliff, P. R.		02/11
CPL	Harding, R. M.		02/11
CPL	Heinemann, A. A.		39/04
PVT	Reed, J.		04/06
PVT	Roeder, J. A.		03/02
PVT	Heller, F.		02/07
PVT	Greenhood, T.		02/07
PVT	Parkhurst, L. B.		02/07
PVT	Greene, W.		02/00
PVT	League, H. M.		02/07
PVT	Arney, E. H.		04/05
PVT	Gormley, H. B.		02/06
PVT	Jandorf, M. F.		00/07
PVT	Fowler, Fred		02/06
PVT	Hoeflich, G. W.		02/07
PVT	McCarthy, C. D.		00/10
PVT	Joyce, T.		02/11
PVT	Hoy, W.		02/04
PVT	Parrish, L. E.		00/10
PVT	Curry, C. E.		02/11
PVT	Christopher, T. J.		02/11
PVT	Cavalien, L. H.		02/11
PVT	Bufter, W. S.		00/11
PVT	Steiner, W. L.		02/06
PVT	Zentgraf, Joseph F.		02/11
PVT	White, N. W.		02/08
PVT	Klingmeyer, H. W.		02/07
PVT	Simmons, Frank H.		02/04
PVT	Roseway, Adam J.		00/01

PVT	Wright, Walter C.		02/10
PVT	Downs, D.		03/00
PVT	Slonaker, Harry B.		02/10
PVT	Eaton, G.	Current enlistment began NOV 1903.	00/00
PVT	Hurt, W.	Current enlistment began JUN 1903.	00/00
PVT	Miller, L. A.	Enlisted 14 FEB 1904.	00/00
PVT	Moyrich, R. F.	Enlisted 11 FEB 1904.	00/00
PVT	Watson, L. H.	Current enlistment began JUN 1901.	00/00
PVT	Lewis, H. C.		08/00

Company C

2LT	Leimbach, George C.	Company Commander. Listed on B CO payroll 16-18 FEB. Transferred to E CO on 18 FEB. Listed on E CO payroll 19-23 FEB.	04/05
1SG	Smith, Charles W.	First Sergeant.	01/01
SGT	Clark, Charles L.	Listed on D CO payroll 16-22 FEB.	03/11
SGT	Kearney, J.	Listed on L CO payroll 16-23 FEB.	04/09
SGT	Anacker, William		03/00
SGT	Price, John W.	Listed on E CO payroll 16-22 FEB.	03/00
SGT	Hoffman, Edmund H.		05/05
CPL	Clazey, William		02/11
CPL	Mitchell, Joseph B.		02/11
CPL	Bennett, Anthony W.		03/01
CPL	Sneed, Harry B.	Paid $1.25/day as CPL 7-15 FEB, paid $1.00/day as PVT and listed on M CO payroll 17-23 FEB.	00/11
CPL	Keenan, Frank	Listed on L CO payroll 16-23 FEB.	02/04
CPL	Moore, August	Listed on L CO payroll 16-23 FEB.	03/05
CPL	Isaac, Gilbert		04/01
CPL	Weissenborn, Fred M.		02/11
PVT	Burton, Guy	Listed on L CO payroll 16-18 FEB.	01/03
PVT	Keys, Herbert	Listed on L CO payroll 16-23 FEB.	02/11
PVT	Beatty, Henry C.		01/01
PVT	Riley, John E.	Listed on B CO payroll 16-23 FEB.	00/11
PVT	Bull, Oscar	Listed on M CO payroll 17-23 FEB.	02/10
PVT	Swain, James E.	Listed on D CO payroll 16-22 FEB.	14/09
PVT	Hultz, Harry		02/09
PVT	Kone, Walter H.		03/00

PVT	Cassell, William H.	Listed on E CO payroll 16-22 FEB.	12.04
PVT	Helfrich, Anthony C.		03/01
PVT	Herkorn, William H.		00/10
PVT	Vessel, George H.	Listed on L CO payroll 16-23 FEB.	00/10
PVT	Warkmeister, Louis		05/03
PVT	Anacker, Herman F.	Listed on L CO payroll 16-23 FEB.	02/09
PVT	Compton, Arch		00/08
PVT	List, Oscar C.	Listed on L CO payroll 16-23 FEB.	00/02
PVT	Adams, Frank H.	Listed on M CO payroll 17-23 FEB.	00/03
PVT	Davis, Warner		00/02
PVT	Kernan, Charles L.		00/02
PVT	Parks, J. Magness		00/01
PVT	Burgess, William H., Jr.	Enlisted 9 FEB 1904. Listed on M CO payroll 17-23 FEB.	00/00
PVT	Schaeffer, Charles F., Jr.	Enlisted 9 FEB 1904. Listed on M CO payroll 16-23 FEB.	00/00

Company D

CPT	Keyes, J. Clifton	Company Commander.	14/08
1LT	Wessels, A. L., MD.	Company Executive Officer.	00/09
1SG	Hummel, George E.	First Sergeant.	11/10
SGT	George, C. H.		06/04
SGT	Williams, C. H.		04/04
SGT	Rice, L.		15/09
CPL	Hickman, Harry S.		04/09
CPL	Jacobson, John		02/11
CPL	Windle, John M.		03/04
CPL	Ruby, Charles F.		03/02
CPL	Staubs, Jesse L.		03/02
CPL	Hayden, Clarence		03/00
CPL	Newton, Howard H.	Total service not listed.	00/00
CPL	Hiltner, John F.		05/04
PVT	Moore, H.	Enlisted 28 MAY 1903.	00/07
PVT	Adams, C. J.		00/09
PVT	Butler, Albert		03/00
PVT	Bottorf, Benjaman F.		00/09
PVT	Hayes, J. S.		00/08

PVT	Hoffman, John M.		00/08
PVT	Degel, Charles		00/08
PVT	Jacobson, Walter S.	Enlisted 11 FEB 1904.	00/00
PVT	Degel, Henry		00/08
PVT	Kohler, Harry C.		01/01
PVT	Eisel, Fred		00/08
PVT	Maykrantz, Albert		02/11
PVT	Hepburn, George L.		00/08
PVT	Norris, Harry		02/11
PVT	Beadenkoff, William P.		03/08
PVT	Fairbanks, Wilbur		05/11
PVT	Hudgins, George		00/08
PVT	Hargrove, William		02/11
PVT	Dailey, H.	Signed with an "X."	06/11
PVT	Reese, George		00/09
PVT	Shanks, Walter L.		02/00
PVT	Tracey, E. C.		01/03
PVT	Trescott, Joseph		00/02
PVT	Walling, Harry		00/08
PVT	Doster, C.		00/08
PVT	Hartzel, W. J.		02/11
PVT	Hammon, F.		01/00
PVT	Hastings, A.	Signed with an "X."	00/08
PVT	Jacobson, John		02/11
PVT	Ouesta, J.		01/00
PVT	Beale, L.		00/11
PVT	Sauks (Sanks), E. L.		02/11
PVT	Shelley, H.		00/08
PVT	Wilkinson, F.		00/02
PVT	Combs, James		00/08
PVT	Peters, J.		01/01
PVT	Wiesenborn, F.	Signed with an "X."	02/00

Company E

CPT	Gill, Albert S.	Company Commander.	06/04
1LT	Knapp, William G.	Company Executive Officer.	01/00
2LT	Richardson, John V.	Died of pneumonia 22 FEB 1904.	00/07
1SG	Redner, Herman C.	First Sergeant.	05/10
SGT	Schiere, Joseph L.		08/07
SGT	Donohue, J. W.		05/06
SGT	Krastell, Joseph		00/03
SGT	Loane, Joseph		05/10
SGT	Schine (Shire), Joseph L.		08/07
CPL	Burnett, H. C.		05/06
CPL	Fowler, George		03/00
CPL	Warfield, Leroy C.		00/10
CPL	Zipprian, Edward		01/11
CPL	Hubley, Clyde W.		03/01
PVT	Armstrong, William E.	Listed as PVT on E CO payroll 7-15 FEB and as CPL on E CO payroll 16-22 FEB.	04/01
PVT	Bauge, George		01/04
PVT	Brent, Edward		02/07
PVT	Brenton, Wallace C.		00/08
PVT	Drexel, Robert		03/00
PVT	Drexel, Walter		00/08
PVT	Darr, J. William		02/07
PVT	Georges, Joseph M.		02/07
PVT	George, Stephen H.		01/04
PVT	George, Howard		00/07
PVT	Marshall, Harry		00/01
PVT	Ironmonger, Charles H.		00/01
PVT	Groverman, Arthur		00/07
PVT	Jones, George		03/00
PVT	Hardy, John		00/07
PVT	Neubert, Joseph L.		01/10
PVT	Killmeyer, Robert M.		01/10
PVT	Oliver, Harry M.		00/07

PVT	Little, Clarence J.		04/07
PVT	Peck, Emil		01/11
PVT	Gladstone, Charles		03/07
PVT	Hanson, Walter S.	Paid $1.10/day 7-15 FEB and paid $1.00/day 16-22 FEB.	03/01
PVT	Killmeyer, Fred		00/07
PVT	Mercer, George P.		01/02
PVT	Hayes, John T.		03/00
PVT	Peters, Charles J.		00/07
PVT	Rourke, Frank		03/00
PVT	Rathbun, H. J.		00/08
PVT	Staylor, John S.		00/07
PVT	Trott, S. W.		00/07
PVT	Vollman, Walter		00/07
PVT	Windle, Ed		00/07
PVT	Baxter, William		00/09
PVT	Schafer (Schaefer), John C.		00/11
PVT	Purnell, Howard T.	Enlisted 14 FEB 1904.	00/00
PVT	Hessler, Emil Edward		01/04
PVT	Morgenroth, H.		02/00
PVT	Jones, A. W.		03/01
PVT	Fitz, E. L.		03/00
PVT	Cole, George E.		02/11
PVT	Hamberry, M. J.		00/08
PVT	Barnes, John		00/08
PVT	Brown, William E.	Previous service in regular army.	00/01
PVT	Dorn, George		01/03
PVT	Jefferson, A.		00/08
PVT	Charlton, W.		00/08
PVT	Bennett, Joseph		02/01

Company F

CPT	Rowe, Moumonier	Company Commander.	00/00
1LT	Gaither, Ernest H.	Company Executive Officer.	01/09
2LT	Cary, French S.		00/01
1SG	Plassil, John	First Sergeant.	06/11

Rank	Name	Notes	Date
SGT	Reilly, J. P.		03/09
SGT	Knight, William C.		03/08
SGT	Chambers, James M.	Listed on H CO payroll 16-22 FEB.	03/10
SGT	Busch, Cornelius		03/09
SGT	Wagner, William C.	Listed on H CO payroll 16-22 FEB.	03/10
CPL	Zimmermann, George H.		03/09
CPL	Koerner (Koener), Edward	Listed on H CO payroll 16-22 FEB.	03/09
CPL	Gillesful, William		03/09
CPL	Gilley, Martin		03/08
CPL	Walstrom, William		03/08
CPL	Bixby, Harry M.		00/01
PVT	Goss, L. V.	Listed on H CO payroll 16-22 FEB.	00/08
PVT	Golden, Joseph	Listed on H CO payroll 16-22 FEB.	00/03
PVT	Brushweller, William J.	Listed on H CO payroll 16-22 FEB.	03/00
PVT	Holland, George F.		00/09
PVT	Brewer, Charles W.	Listed on H CO payroll 16-22 FEB.	00/02
PVT	Horan, James	Listed on H CO payroll 16-22 FEB.	03/00
PVT	Shoppelman (Coppelman), John		03/10
PVT	Johnston, Wilson		00/03
PVT	Fox, Jacob	Listed on H CO payroll 16-22 FEB.	02/08
PVT	Koerner, Henry	Listed on D CO payroll 16-22 FEB.	00/04
PVT	Allen, James H.		00/09
PVT	Bookman, Gust		00/08
PVT	Clark, Lawrence		00/08
PVT	Gilley, George		02/07
PVT	Brewer, Charles E.	Listed on H CO payroll 16-22 FEB.	00/01
PVT	Krause, Rudolph E.		01/01
PVT	Leach (Leech), William	Listed on H CO payroll 16-22 FEB.	03/08
PVT	List, George S.		03/07
PVT	List, Milton	Listed on H CO payroll 16-22 FEB. Paid $1.10/day 7-15 FEB and paid $1.00/day 16-22 FEB.	03/00
PVT	Marley, John		00/08
PVT	Undutch, John	Died of pneumonia 21 FEB 1904.	00/01
PVT	Woods, Harry E.	Listed on H CO payroll 16-22 FEB.	00/01

PVT	Shelton, Ross T.		00/08
PVT	Suter, Clifton		00/08
PVT	Smith, Harry L.	Listed on H CO payroll 16-22 FEB.	03/00
PVT	Reeves, A. J.	Enlisted 2 Feb 1904.	00/00
PVT	Snooks, Harry E.	Listed on D CO payroll 16-22 FEB.	00/08
PVT	Webster, Horace		00/08
PVT	Assner, Allen	Enlisted 12 Feb 1904. Listed on H CO payroll 16-22 FEB.	00/00
PVT	LeCompte, William A. F.	Enlisted 12 Feb 1904. Listed on H CO payroll 16-22 FEB.	00/00
PVT	Arnold, Calvin W.	Enlisted 13 Feb 1904. Listed on H CO payroll 16-22 FEB.	00/00

Company G

1LT	Jones, Harvey L.	Company Commander.	03/07
2LT	Blake, Herbert C.	Executive Officer, G CO. Listed on K CO payroll 16-20 FEB.	00/07
QM	Lauke, Frederick	Quartermaster.	01/11
1SG	Conrad, Schick	First sergeant.	02/00
SGT	Sewell, Joseph C.	Paid $1.50/day 10-15 FEB, paid $1.65/day 16-20 FEB. Listed on K CO payroll 16-20 FEB.	05/11
SGT	Hillman, Harry	Listed on B CO payroll for 16-23 FEB.	00/11
SGT	Rohleder, Thomas J.	Listed on E CO payroll 16-22 FEB.	02/00
SGT	Metovsky, Joseph		02/07
CPL	Bast, Alfred		02/07
CPL	DeBaufre, Berry		04/06
CPL	Heineman, August		03/04
CPL	Litz, George	Enlisted 11 Feb 1904. Listed as PVT and paid $1.00/day 11-15 FEB and listed on K CO payroll 15-20 FEB as CPL paid $1.25/day.	00/00
CPL	Simon, John		02/10
CPL	Stahlkneckt (Stallkneckt), Edward		02/00
CPL	Lewis, Harry		02/00
PVT	Hiltner, Harry		09/07
PVT	Allen, Edward	Listed on B CO payroll 16-23 FEB.	00/08
PVT	Illig, Charles O.	Listed on B CO payroll 16-23 FEB.	04/00
PVT	Bohlman, Henry		00/08
PVT	Jenkins, Robert E.	Listed on B CO payroll 16-23 FEB.	00/08
PVT	Cooper, Arthur M.	Listed on B CO payroll 16-23 FEB.	00/08

PVT	Kane, Oscar	Listed on B CO payroll 16-23 FEB.	01/03
PVT	Eurice (Eurich), George	Listed on B CO payroll 16-23 FEB.	00/08
PVT	Knauff (Knauft), William H.		05/10
PVT	Hirt, William		00/08
PVT	Carter, Charles W.	Listed on B CO payroll 16-23 FEB.	00/08
PVT	Dixon, Ira	Listed on B CO payroll 16-23 FEB.	00/03
PVT	Gladstone, William	Listed on B CO payroll 16-23 FEB.	01/11
PVT	Baerwald, Richard E.		01/04
PVT	Arminger, Henry J.		02/10
PVT	Kriechbaum, George	Listed on B CO payroll 16-23 FEB.	00/08
PVT	Legg, Charles E.		02/08
PVT	Lucas, Joseph S.	Listed on B CO payroll 16-23 FEB.	02/07
PVT	Lipsch, Max		00/08
PVT	Kelly, William	Listed on B CO payroll 16-23 FEB.	00/08
PVT	Shipley, Edward A.		00/11
PVT	Magereth, Henry H.		02/00
PVT	Schleuther, Herman	Listed on B CO payroll 16-23 FEB.	00/08
PVT	O'Brien, Philip E.	Listed on B CO payroll 16-23 FEB.	00/08
PVT	Stapf, George W.		00/08
PVT	Rever, Frederick		01/04
PVT	Turner, William F.	Enlisted 11 FEB 1904.	00/00
PVT	Sebald, Philipp	Listed on B CO payroll 16-23 FEB.	00/01
PVT	Myrick, Robert (Richard) F.	Enlisted 11 FEB 1904.	00/00
PVT	O'Brien, Thomas F.	Listed on B CO payroll 16-23 FEB.	00/08
PVT	Rose, William F.		01/03
PVT	Smith, Sidney		00/01
PVT	Wolf, Edward	Listed on B CO payroll 16-23 FEB.	00/08
PVT	Wilson, Charles H.	Listed on B CO payroll 16-23 FEB.	00/08
PVT	Zollinhofer, William	Listed on B CO payroll 16-23 FEB.	00/03

Company H

CPT	Gootee, Brice B.	Company Commander.	04/03
1LT	Sherman, A. K.	Company Executive Officer.	13/03
2LT	Duce, Charles K.		06/04
1SG	Debring, Walter R.	First Sergeant.	04/05

SGT	Bennett, Edwin J.		07/01
SGT	Wachter (Wachner), Edward J.		04/01
SGT	Kelly, Thomas F.		04/05
SGT	Bussell, John M.		03/11
CPL	Stewart, L. R.		03/00
CPL	Burus, Milton R.		02/11
CPL	Wheeler, Charles H.		00/11
CPL	Hudgins, Charles J.	Paid $1.25/day 7-15 FEB and paid $1.38/day 16-22 FEB.	03/00
CPL	Hull, Samuel W.		00/09
CPL	Burns, Milton R.		02/11
CPL	Gillespie, William		03/09
PVT	Ayers, James A.		00/08
PVT	Banks (Barry), Albert	Clerk spells last name "Banks," signature appears to be "Barry."	00/08
PVT	Bell, Samuel K.		00/08
PVT	Burneston, William N.		04/09
PVT	Burke, Harry W.		00/08
PVT	Emery, Oliver		00/08
PVT	Emerich, William V.		00/10
PVT	Fischer, J. F. Albert		00/08
PVT	Mister, John William		02/07
PVT	Arring, James W.	Enlisted 7 FEB 1904.	00/00
PVT	Kramer, Charles H., Jr.		02/07
PVT	Beckett, Thomas M. O.		00/08
PVT	Krug, Henry G.		03/08
PVT	Linke, John H.		00/08
PVT	Pyle, William J.		03/00
PVT	Magness, John	Enlisted 7 FEB 1904.	00/00
PVT	Quillen, James H.		00/08
PVT	Askey, William M.		00/08
PVT	Riley, Herbert		02/07
PVT	Robertson, H. E.		02/09
PVT	Walterhofer, Charles G. (S.)		02/07
PVT	Wanner, Arthur H.		00/07

PVT	White, Andrew J. C.		00/07
PVT	Karcher, Alfred G.		03/05
PVT	Kane, James F.		00/08
PVT	Hardesty, James M.		00/02
PVT	Green, Bernard		01/02
PVT	Gillespie, James T., Jr.		00/08
PVT	Schmidt, William		00/03
PVT	Henkelmann, Edward		06/08
PVT	Pfanmuller (Pfaninueler), Henry F.		03/10
PVT	Reinfelder, Joseph J.		01/08
PVT	Vogel, Henry		02/07
PVT	Wooden, James H.		03/00
PVT	Treffinger, H. H.		01/01
PVT	Lambert, Arthur		02/07

Company I

1LT	Rittenhouse, J. E.	Company Commander.	12/10
1SG	Paisal, W. Vernon	First Sergeant I CO. Listed on M CO payroll as SGT, paid $1.82/day 17-23 FEB.	08/09
SGT	Muth, John A.	Listed on D CO payroll 16-22 FEB.	08/10
SGT	Barrett, Samuel G.	Listed on K CO payroll 16-20 FEB.	12/01
SGT	Wain, Charles W.	Listed on M CO payroll 17-23 FEB.	10/10
SGT	Bruce, James G.		06/10
CPL	Gibson, George G.		06/10
CPL	Rupp, Frederick W.	Listed on E CO payroll 16-22 FEB.	04/03
CPL	McCurley, James B.	Listed on M CO payroll 16-23 FEB.	04/01
CPL	Donnelly, James E.	Paid $1.25/day as CPL 7-15 FEB, paid $1.00/day as PVT and listed on M CO payroll 16-23 FEB.	02/07
CPL	Healey, William J.	Listed on M CO payroll 16-23 FEB.	02/11
PVT	Arnold, Edward S.		01/02
PVT	Atkinson, Warren		01/02
PVT	Bloom, Isaac		01/00
PVT	Weber, Mervin	Listed on L CO payroll 16-23 FEB.	00/11
PVT	Young, Benjamin G.	Listed on M CO payroll 17-23 FEB.	01/01
PVT	Dawson, Edward W.		01/03
PVT	Zeller, Joseph	Listed on M CO payroll 17-23 FEB.	00/11

PVT	Fendley, John W., Jr.		03/06
PVT	Higgenbothom (Higgenbottom), Charles H.	Enlisted 2 FEB 1904. Listed on M CO payroll 16-23 FEB.	00/00
PVT	Hobbs, Osborn		02/07
PVT	Haney, Walter J.	Enlisted 2 FEB 1904. Listed on M CO payroll 17-23 FEB.	00/00
PVT	Kelly, James		01/00
PVT	Obitz, Lawrence	Enlisted 2 FEB 1904.	00/00
PVT	Lowry, John		02/11
PVT	Smith, Charles H.	Enlisted 2 FEB 1904. Listed on D CO payroll 16-22 FEB.	00/00
PVT	McAllister, Frank	Listed on M CO payroll 17-23 FEB.	00/03
PVT	Freeman, William H. (Ed)	Enlisted 2 FEB 1904. Signed "Wm H. Freeman" on I CO payroll 15 FEB, signed "Ed Freeman" on M CO payroll 17-23 FEB. Same handwriting, identical enlistment date.	00/00
PVT	Newton, Henry J.	Listed on D CO payroll 16-22	00/11
PVT	Lemkes, H. (Hamond)		01/01
PVT	Hines, James W.		01/00
PVT	Wain, Howard	Listed on M CO payroll 17-23 FEB.	02/11
PVT	Wehrenberg, Fred	Listed on M CO payroll 17-23 FEB.	00/08
PVT	Conaway, William		01/00
PVT	Staubs, Robert C.	Listed on M CO payroll 17-23 FEB.	01/02
PVT	Weidenheimer, George		03/00
PVT	Hickman, Herbert D.		02/10
PVT	Layton, Arthur C. (Charles A.)	Listed on M CO payroll 17-23 FEB.	01/02
PVT	Martin, Robert C.	Listed on M CO payroll 17-23 FEB.	03/01
PVT	McCurley, William	Listed on M CO payroll 17-23 FEB.	03/00
PVT	Schnebelen, Edward	Listed on M CO payroll 17-23 FEB.	02/08

Company K

CPT	Haynes, Harry E.	Company Commander.	14/05
1LT	Hummel, Charles E.	Company Executive Officer.	12/09
2LT	Holland, John Leo		03/10
1SG	Jacobs, John R.	First Sergeant.	06/10
SGT	Saxton, Oscar	Quartermaster Sergeant.	09/10
SGT	Staisloff, Charles		03/10
SGT	Knauff, Joseph		05/10

Rank	Name	Notes	Days
CPL	Von Hagel, Charles		05/08
CPL	Weilbenner, Louis		01/09
CPL	Trimble, Walter		00/10
CPL	Upton, John	Paid $1.67/day 7-15 FEB, paid $1.52/day 16-20 FEB.	14/07
CPL	Lingerman, Louis		03/10
PVT	Andrews, William B.		03/02
PVT	Calwel, George		02/11
PVT	Wayne, James		00/08
PVT	Ripplemeyer, Leo		03/01
PVT	Von Hagel, William		02/11
PVT	Merten, George		02/11
PVT	Burkhead, William		00/10
PVT	Rider, John		02/09
PVT	Greenhood, L.		00/08
PVT	Miller, Samuel		01/11
PVT	Eliason, C.		02/11
PVT	McKenna, William J.		01/00
PVT	McCaull, J. A.		03/10
PVT	Hollan, J.		02/11
PVT	Crawford, A.		01/11
PVT	Lutz, Walter		02/07
PVT	Fowler, John J.	Enlisted 14 FEB 1904.	00/00
PVT	Brown, C. P.		00/11
PVT	Reeb (Reib), John		02/08
PVT	Volanfer (Volaufer), George W.		02/11
PVT	Cole, Frank	Enlisted 15 FEB 1904.	00/00
PVT	Jenkins, C. F.	Enlisted 16 FEB 1904.	00/00
PVT	Lowery, Joseph	Enlisted 16 FEB 1904.	00/00
PVT	King, John	Enlisted 15 FEB 1904.	00/00
PVT	Rooney, William	Enlisted 16 FEB 1904.	00/00
PVT	Bohlmann, Henry	Enlisted 16 FEB 1904.	00/00
PVT	Emge	Enlisted 16 FEB 1904. Listed on K CO payroll 16-20 FEB as "In City Jail." This is probably PVT Harry Embe who was arrested with PVT Edward Meyers for stealing a fire extinguisher. For more information, see PVT Edward Meyers' record.	00/00

PVT	Donahue, E. J.	Enlisted 16 FEB 1904.	00/00
PVT	Miller, H.	Enlisted 16 FEB 1904.	00/00
PVT	Hutchins, S. J.	Enlisted 16 FEB 1904.	00/00
PVT	Allen, Frank	Enlisted 16 FEB 1904.	00/00
PVT	Scott, R.	Enlisted 16 FEB 1904.	00/00
PVT	Frank, George	Enlisted 15 FEB 1904.	00/00
PVT	McNue, Cla.	Enlisted 16 FEB 1904.	00/00
PVT	Simmon, John	Enlisted 15 FEB 1904.	00/00
PVT	Cooper, C.		00/09
PVT	Hauser, William	Enlisted 16 FEB 1904.	00/00
PVT	Young, (Joe?)	Enlisted 15 FEB 1904.	00/00
PVT	Ahring, W.	Enlisted 16 FEB 1904.	00/00
PVT	Sachs, (Abe?)	Enlisted 16 FEB 1904.	00/00
PVT	Johnson, George	Enlisted 16 FEB 1904.	00/00
PVT	Mayers, Charles	Enlisted 16 FEB 1904. Listed on L CO payroll 22-23 FEB.	00/00
PVT	Hoffman, William	Enlisted 6 FEB 1904.	00/00
PVT	Slone, Henry	Enlisted 18 FEB 1904.	00/00
PVT	Chambers, George	Enlisted 18 FEB 1904.	00/00
PVT	Merchant, Frank	Enlisted 18 FEB 1904.	00/00
PVT	Thompson, E.	Enlisted 18 FEB 1904.	00/00

Company L

CPT	Stesch, Ed. H. J.	Company Commander.	34/00
1LT	Frittita, Joseph	Company Executive Officer.	07/04
2LT	Voneiff, Craft W.		01/03
1SG	Schmidt, John H.	First Sergeant.	07/04
SGT	Bora, Antony (Toni)	Paid $1.82/day as SGT 7-15 FEB, paid $2.12/day as 1SG 16-23 FEB.	07/01
SGT	Hoefer (Hofer), Walter		06/10
SGT	Cadell, Samuel J.		03/00
SGT	Lewis, D. C.		03/04
SGT	Hoffman, C.		05/04
CPL	Hall, Edward J.		04/05
CPL	Briscoe, F. B.		05/01
CPL	Devine, Edward J.		04/10
CPL	Carr, John R.		01/04

PVT	Reinecke, William H.		03/01
PVT	Abicht, Robert		03/00
PVT	Rose, Lewis		03/00
PVT	Rockel, George		01/01
PVT	Coligi, Raffala (Raphael)		01/02
PVT	Birkholz, Harry		00/08
PVT	Bora, Fillip		03/00
PVT	Warner, W.		03/00
PVT	Rockel, August		01/00
PVT	Witzgall, Walter		02/08
PVT	Lloyd, Daugherty		00/03
PVT	Schiminger, John C.		00/08
PVT	Iseralson, Michel		02/01
PVT	Smith, Arthur		00/08
PVT	Hill, William H.		00/08
PVT	Brooks, Robert		03/00
PVT	Hall, Walter C.		00/08
PVT	Walker, Joe		00/08
PVT	Scott, Robert J.		00/08
PVT	Rosenthal (Rozenthal), William B.		01/03
PVT	Davis, George		00/02
PVT	White, John L.		00/09
PVT	Hamilton, Samuel	Company cook.	03/00
PVT	Gibson, William H.		01/06
PVT	Golden, David		03/00
PVT	Fowler, Charles W.		01/11
PVT	Forvitz, Harry J.		03/00
PVT	Hirkomer (Hirkorm), William H.		01/01
PVT	Holtz, H.		02/10
PVT	Allen, Thomas S.		03/10
PVT	Freberger, Caswell B.	Enlisted 17 FEB 1904.	00/00
PVT	Ross, Frank	Enlisted 17 FEB 1904.	00/00
PVT	Lunder (Lender), Charles	Enlisted 17 FEB 1904.	00/00

Company M

CPT	Filbert, Samuel W.	Company Commander.	12/05
1LT	Lyman, Albert E.	Company Executive Officer.	17/11
2LT	Tavenner, M. (Michael) K.		06/00
1SG	McCeney, Jacob	First Sergeant.	07/10
1SG	Sylvester, William W.	Paid $1.82/day and listed as SGT 7-15 FEB, paid $2.12/day and listed as 1SG 16-23 FEB.	07/08
SGT	Connor, Albert R.		09/07
SGT	Marley, John		07/08
SGT	Duvall, Charles S.		07/08
SGT	Smith, L.		01/06
CPL	Worstman, Frank		01/01
CPL	Pines, William		05/10
CPL	Vogeler, Fred	Paid $1.38/day as CPL 7-15 FEB, paid $1.10/day as PVT 17-23 FEB.	04/01
CPL	Applegarth, William		05/10
CPL	Hasselberg, Fred		03/10
CPL	Van Stavonen, James E.		04/00
CPL	Boyd, Charles		03/09
CPL	Hellen, Charles		04/02
CPL	Pines, Alex		04/05
PVT	Tegeler (Tegelir), Albert		00/08
PVT	Shipley, Harry		00/08
PVT	Seward, Edward		00/10
PVT	Stonesifer, Edward		01/11
PVT	Williams, Edward		00/08
PVT	Williams, Benjamin C.		00/10
PVT	Lee, Charles A.		00/04
PVT	Dunker, Harry J.		00/02
PVT	Carroll, A. F.		00/08
PVT	Dorr, Joseph		03/01
PVT	Carre, Clarence		00/02
PVT	Block, Harry		02/07
PVT	Aidt, Louis		01/01
PVT	Arminger, Sidney		00/08

PVT	Jones, Oliver		00/08
PVT	Mehrbrei, Michael A.		00/08
PVT	McCabe, James		03/02
PVT	Markel, William		01/00
PVT	Miller, George		00/03
PVT	Hartzell, Milton E.		00/10
PVT	Knell, Joseph K.		02/08
PVT	Morrison, David		02/02
PVT	Allen, William G.	Enlisted 2 FEB 1904.	00/00
PVT	Kermet, Fred O.	Enlisted 2 FEB 1904.	00/00
PVT	Cumberland, William	Enlisted 2 FEB 1904.	00/00
PVT	Davis, William		00/03
PVT	Schwartz, William		00/08
PVT	Workmeister, Louis		05/06
PVT	Meeks, Herbert F.		03/01
PVT	Lucas, H.		03/03

Fifth Regiment, Infantry

Headquarters and Staff

COL	Warfield, Henry Mactier	Regimental Commander.	18/04
MAJ	Spruill, St. Clair	Surgeon.	00/08
MAJ	Rawlins, Louis M.	Provisional Battalion Commander.	15/10
MAJ	Miller, Robert J.	Quartermaster.	33/02
MAJ	Johnson, E. C.	Commissary Officer.	36/10
MAJ	Hinkley, John		19/07
MAJ	Clotworthy, C. Baker		15/11
CPT	Davis, S. G., Jr.	Assistant Surgeon.	13/03
CPT	Dame, W. M.	Chaplain. Payroll clerk indicated Dame was included by "mistake" and was not paid.	14/07
CPT	Keyser, Henry B.	Ordnance Officer.	18/00
CPT	Clark, Thaddeus W.	Assistant Surgeon.	05/10
CPT	Pope, Micajah W.	Provost Marshall.	00/02
CPT	Poe, R. Johnson	Adjutant.	19/07
1LT	Hutton, H. M.	Adjutant Officer.	11/10
1LT	Holmes, W. Pinkney	Adjutant Officer. Listed as Quartermaster-Commissary Officer 16-23 FEB.	13/03

1LT	Bryan, Carryl H.	Retired. Listed as acting Commissary and Quartermaster Officer, 7-15 FEB; and as acting Paymaster 16-23 FEB.	12/11
LTC	Coale, R. Dorsey	Regimental Executive Officer.	17/05
LT	Turner, George J.	Adjutant Officer.	06/07
LT	Glocker, Albert E.	Retired. Acting Commissary and Quartermaster Officer.	15/00
SGM	Gorman, B. J.	Battalion Sergeant Major.	03/07
SGM	Lottes, Louis	Battalion Sergeant Major.	10/01
SGM	O'Conner, Fergus	Regimental Sergeant Major.	36/09
SGM	Johnson, George D.	Battalion Sergeant Major.	17/05
SGT	Anderson, H. W.		36/10
SGT	Kaesemeyer, George W.	Ordnance Sergeant.	21/07
SGT	Putsche, Thomas F.	Quartermaster Sergeant.	16/06
SGT	Duval, E. B.	Commissary Sergeant.	27/05
SGT	Gruss, Fred A.	Listed as Color Sergeant 7-15 FEB and as Quartermaster Sergeant 16-23 FEB.	23/03
SGT	Dogge, Albert H.	Listed as Color Sergeant 7-15 FEB and as Commissary Sergeant 16-21 FEB. Listed on B CO payroll 22-23 FEB.	00/07
	Ashbury, Howard E.	Hospital Steward.	02/03
	Callahan, Thomas D.	Hospital Steward.	02/07
	Shipley, Arthur H.	Hospital Steward.	00/01
	Czarnowsky, Herbert (F.)	Field Musician.	05/08
	Bell, Edward F.	Field Musician.	33/08
	Wynn, Harry L.	Field Musician.	15/08

Company A

CPT	Bowie, Robert B.	Company Commander.	17/09
1LT	Diffenderfer, C. R.	Company Executive Officer. Listed on I CO payroll 16-22 FEB.	09/08
2LT	Brady, Upton S.		07/09
1SG	Baetzer, Charles H.	First Sergeant.	05/11
SGT	Yard, Harold	Listed on I CO payroll 16-22 FEB.	04/09
SGT	Slingluff, (W.)		04/11
SGT	Buchanan, Thomas G.		05/10
SGT	Robbins, Ed, Jr.		03/00
CPL	Slingluff, Horace, Jr.	Listed on I CO payroll 16-22 FEB.	02/11

Rank	Name	Notes	
CPL	Reynolds, Clarence S.	Company Clerk.	03/09
CPL	Templeman, F. Leroy		03/09
CPL	Shepherd, F. B.	Listed on I CO payroll 16-22 FEB.	04/05
CPL	Duer, Harry Lay		04/05
CPL	Kirkwood, Thomas	Listed on I CO payroll 16-22 FEB.	03/05
CPL	Atkinson, M. S., Jr.		03/01
CPL	Gaither, H. W., Jr.		04/05
PVT	Bevan, William F.	Listed on I CO payroll 16-22 FEB.	00/05
PVT	Freeman, D. S.		02/04
PVT	Jenkins, Charles R.	Listed on I CO payroll 16-22 FEB.	01/04
PVT	Lyon, J. W., Jr.		01/10
PVT	Cushing, W. W.	Signed with an "X."	00/04
PVT	Henry, Adkins		01/03
PVT	Keating, B. P., Jr.		01/01
PVT	Duvall, W. P.		00/03
PVT	Dukehart, J. Krebs		02/01
PVT	Boyce, A. P.		02/04
PVT	Jenkins, W. (Q.)		00/03
PVT	Slingluff, D. H.	Listed on I CO payroll 16-22 FEB.	00/04
PVT	Stump, J. S., Jr.	Listed on I CO payroll 16-22 FEB.	00/03
PVT	Browne, H. A.	Listed on I CO payroll 16-22 FEB.	01/10
PVT	Dukehart, J. A. B.	Listed on I CO payroll 16-22 FEB.	00/02
PVT	Hollingsworth, R. J.	Listed on I CO payroll 16-22 FEB.	00/04
PVT	Palmer, R. McGill	Listed on I CO payroll 16-22 FEB.	00/03
PVT	Pomelle, Edward B.		00/03
PVT	Patterson, John H.		02/04
PVT	Painter, L. G.		02/11
PVT	Riggs, Laurie H.	Listed on I CO payroll 16-22 FEB.	00/09
PVT	Owen, F. Buchanan		02/08
PVT	Mason, Steven Thomson	Listed on I CO payroll 16-22 FEB.	02/04
PVT	Marye, R. Turner	Listed on I CO payroll 16-22 FEB.	00/10
PVT	Levering, H. Brooke	Listed on I CO payroll 16-21 FEB.	00/10
PVT	Levering, F. A., Jr.	Listed on I CO payroll 16-22 FEB.	02/04
PVT	Lowndes, Charles H. G.	Enlisted 12 FEB 1904. Listed on I CO payroll 16-22 FEB.	00/00

PVT	Wilmer, J. C.	Enlisted 12 FEB 1904. Listed on I CO payroll 16-22 FEB.	00/00
PVT	Shaffer, Luther Porter	Enlisted 12 FEB 1904. Listed on I CO payroll 16-22 FEB.	00/00

Company B

CPT	Janney, Thomas S.	Company Commander.	12/11
1LT	Daly, Henry T.	Company Executive Officer.	24/02
1SG	Bauer, C. A.	First Sergeant.	13/02
SGT	Stewart, L. H.		06/11
SGT	Reed, J. B. T.		07/01
SGT	Dukehart, M. J.		05/09
SGT	Scott, J. W.	Quartermaster Sergeant.	06/11
CPL	George, Barry		02/11
CPL	Laroque, J. M.		03/02
CPL	Berry, R. B.		01/04
CPL	Thompson, B. M.		02/10
CPL	Dukehart, G. J.		03/01
PVT	Catheart, H. G.		02/10
PVT	Derr, F. L.		04/01
PVT	Dukehart, H. P.	Enlisted 25 JAN 1904.	00/00
PVT	Dwyer, Paul P.		02/11
PVT	Eckstein, Albert		00/09
PVT	Laib, F. K.		02/08
PVT	Lawrence, Harry C.		00/02
PVT	Gosnell, John T.		02/04
PVT	Middlekauff, H. D.		02/11
PVT	Griffith, Carroll S.	Enlisted 10 FEB 1904.	00/00
PVT	Minton, J. L.		00/10
PVT	Knoche, Frank		00/08
PVT	Piehler, F. W.		00/08
PVT	Krieg, Charles		00/03
PVT	Percival, James J.		00/02
PVT	Fisher, B. F.		00/08
PVT	Hanson, W. Ward	Enlisted 10 FEB 1904.	00/00
PVT	Krentzer, C. R.		00/04
PVT	List, S. E.		02/11

PVT	Goodrich (Goodrick), E. M.		00/08
PVT	Prather, J. B., Jr.		02/11
PVT	Smith, A. H.		00/10
PVT	Wirth, G. G., Jr.		01/11
PVT	Watson, D. B.		00/02
PVT	Weber, Abram		00/02
PVT	Klimm, George		00/02
PVT	Bishop, John T.		07/07
PVT	Claypoole, William		05/08
PVT	Bareford, J. T.		01/02
CIV	Bundy, C. S.	Cook. Employed 17-23 FEB.	

Company C

CPT	Thomson, Elbert	Company Commander.	12/09
1LT	Ridgely, G. W.	Company Executive Officer.	07/11
2LT	Streett, E. O.		07/10
1SG	Morgenroth, Oscar	First Sergeant.	09/10
SGT	Woodey, John F.	Listed on L CO payroll 16-23 FEB.	06/04
SGT	Alexander, William W.		04/09
SGT	Cooke, F. D.		04/04
SGT	Truitt, J. H.	Listed on I CO payroll 16-22 FEB.	05/10
SGT	Fisher, Winfield	Quartermaster Sergeant.	14/04
CPL	Ernst, William F.	Listed on L CO payroll 16-23 FEB.	05/09
CPL	Bowen, James H.		05/11
CPL	Knoerr, Jacob	Listed on L CO payroll 16-23 FEB.	11/11
CPL	Langford, C. A.		03/04
CPL	Bechtel, R. II.		02/11
CPL	Smith, E. A.		01/08
PVT	Bechtel, G. K.		00/09
PVT	Blum, Frank		00/08
PVT	Childs, George	Listed on L CO payroll 16-23 FEB.	00/04
PVT	Jones, Frank H.	Listed on L CO payroll 16-23 FEB.	03/09
PVT	Kachner, J. F.		02/09
PVT	Ernst, F. J.	Listed on L CO payroll 16-23 FEB.	00/08
PVT	Kamphaus, August	Listed on L CO payroll 16-23 FEB.	02/11
PVT	Feldpusch, Ferdinand	Listed on L CO payroll 16-23 FEB.	00/09

PVT	Kansler, William H.	Enlisted 7 FEB 1904.	00/00
PVT	Gewecke, Charles H.		06/00
PVT	Kelly, William L.	Listed on L CO payroll 16-23 FEB.	01/04
PVT	Hopper, C. D.	Listed on L CO payroll 16-23 FEB.	02/11
PVT	Kohl, John J.	Listed on L CO payroll 16-23 FEB.	06/00
PVT	Edell, D. J.	Listed on L CO payroll 16-23 FEB.	00/10
PVT	Fox, G. F.		07/01
PVT	Hall, S. G.		03/08
PVT	Hyman, Clarence E.	Listed on L CO payroll 16-23 FEB.	01/04
PVT	Falk, Paul	Listed on L CO payroll 16-23 FEB.	00/08
PVT	Lockwood, Frank		01/03
PVT	Long, C. Arthur		03/00
PVT	McDonald, Edward	Listed on L CO payroll 16-23 FEB.	02/10
PVT	McWhirter, Edgar		00/09
PVT	Mangold, William	Listed on L CO payroll 16-23 FEB.	05/10
PVT	Mordecai, William C.		05/09
PVT	Stump, E. A.		02/11
PVT	Newton, J. E.		00/09
PVT	Thompson, H. F.		05/10
PVT	O'Brien, William W.		00/09
PVT	Ward, Hamlet	Listed on L CO payroll 16-23 FEB.	07/06
PVT	Russell, Edward H.	Listed on L CO payroll 16-23 FEB.	00/10
PVT	Denmead, Arthur R.	Listed on L CO payroll 16-23 FEB.	00/08
PVT	Schultz, Charles H.		06/02
PVT	Dooley, W. J.	Enlisted 13 FEB 1904. Listed on L CO payroll 16-19 FEB.	00/00
PVT	Smithson, Ivan	Listed on L CO payroll 21-22 FEB.	00/08
PVT	Peregoy, Wilbur B.	Listed on L CO payroll 16-23 FEB.	01/00
PVT	Samsell, John M.		01/04
PVT	Sheridan, J. Robert	Listed on L CO payroll 16-23 FEB.	00/04
PVT	Nusz, H. F.		01/11
PVT	Hobbs, James C.	Listed on I CO payroll 16-22 FEB.	00/03
PVT	Greves, David W.	Listed on L CO payroll 16-23 FEB.	03/05

Company D

Rank	Name	Notes	
CPT	Markoe, John S.	Company Commander, D CO. Listed on B CO payroll 22-23 FEB.	10/00
2LT	Younger, Thomas J.	Company Executive Officer, D CO. Listed on B CO payroll 16-23 FEB.	11/11
1SG	Livingston, Harry C.	First Sergeant. Listed on B CO payroll 16-23 FEB.	22/04
SGT	McNemar, Oscar		06/03
SGT	Erler, George R.		08/05
SGT	Old, F. E.		04/08
SGT	Frey, William W. B.	Listed on B CO payroll 16-23 FEB.	10/03
SGT	Ritter, Leopold J.	Quartermaster Sergeant.	14/11
CPL	Cockrill, H. C.		13/11
CPL	Stevenson, John J.	Paid $1.52/day 7-15 FEB and $1.38/day 16-23 FEB. Listed on B CO payroll 16-23 FEB.	08/04
CPL	Kerchner, F. W.	Listed on I CO payroll 18-22 FEB.	02/00
CPL	Snyder, Harry E.	Listed on B CO payroll 16-23 FEB.	03/02
CPL	Byrnes, W. A.		02/09
PVT	Allard, C. G.	Listed on B CO payroll 16-23 FEB.	02/11
PVT	Bell, W. A.	Listed on L CO payroll 16-23 FEB.	01/03
PVT	Blair, William H.	Listed on B CO payroll 17-23 FEB.	00/09
PVT	Bladin, C. E.	Listed on B CO payroll 16-23 FEB.	00/01
PVT	Brown, J. L.	Listed on B CO payroll 16-23 FEB.	00/01
PVT	Bowersox, A. E.	Listed on L CO payroll 16-23 FEB.	00/09
PVT	Bereford, J. T.	Signed with an "X."	01/02
PVT	Craggs, R.	Enlisted 11 FEB 1904.	00/00
PVT	Cook, R. R.	Listed on L CO payroll 16-23 FEB.	02/03
PVT	Dougherty, B.	Listed on B CO payroll 16-23 FEB.	05/10
PVT	Donahue, J. A.	Listed on L CO payroll 16-23 FEB.	00/07
PVT	Foreman, A. E.	Listed on L CO payroll 16-23 FEB.	00/07
PVT	Wentworth, S. T.	Enlisted 8 FEB 1904. Listed on B CO payroll 16-23 FEB.	00/00
PVT	Smith, Randolph R.	Listed on B CO payroll 16-23 FEB.	00/01
PVT	Hevie, W.	Enlisted 10 FEB 1904. Listed on B CO payroll 16-23 FEB.	00/00
PVT	Seymore, J. B.		05/09
PVT	Jump, C. H.	Listed on B CO payroll 21-23 FEB.	01/02
PVT	Spamer, J. A.		01/03

PVT	Livingston, George A.		01/03
PVT	Stonesifer, Edward A.	Listed on B CO payroll 16-23 FEB.	00/10
PVT	Robinson, C. H.		00/10
PVT	Snyder, William W.	Listed on B CO payroll 16-23 FEB.	01/01
PVT	Stevenson, James T.		08/01
PVT	Karl, Felix	Enlisted 4 FEB 1904. Listed on B CO payroll 16-23 FEB.	00/00
PVT	Paxon, E. H.	Listed on B CO payroll 16 FEB.	01/02
PVT	Stevenson, William		07/00
PVT	Hamley, L. E.	Listed on B CO payroll 16-23 FEB.	00/07
PVT	Shipley, J. H.	Listed on L CO payroll 16-23 FEB.	00/09
PVT	Sipes, D. L.	Listed on B CO payroll 16-23 FEB.	00/08
PVT	Truman, W. E.	Listed on B CO payroll 16-23 FEB.	02/11
PVT	Whitney, W.		00/07
PVT	Hirth, Daniel	Enlisted 8 FEB 1904. Listed on B CO payroll 16-23 FEB.	00/00

Company E

CPT	Thomas, T. R.	Company Commander.	09/10
1LT	White, James C. (Clinton)	Company Executive Officer.	05/09
2LT	Cooper, C. V. M.		03/09
1SG	Wright, Edwin O.	First Sergeant. Listed on I CO payroll 16-22 FEB.	08/11
SGT	Meisel, Frank N.		08/02
SGT	de Guise, Carroll	Listed on L CO payroll 16-23 FEB.	05/10
SGT	Foreman, Custer B.		04/05
SGT	Wands, H. B.		03/03
SGT	Benson, Charles M.	Quartermaster Sergeant.	04/06
CPL	Green, Edward		04/00
CPL	Bornscheuer, John	Listed on K CO payroll 16-22 FEB.	02/04
CPL	Scott, John C.		02/04
CPL	Thomas, Douglas	Listed on I CO payroll 16-17 FEB.	02/03
CPL	Varian, H. L.		01/04
CPL	Phillips, Harry	Listed on K CO payroll 16-22 FEB.	01/01
PVT	Bornsheuer, Adolph	Listed on K CO payroll 16-22 FEB.	02/03
PVT	Bowen, Howard W.		02/09
PVT	Day, Thomas J.	Listed on K CO payroll 16-22 FEB.	00/08

PVT	Dryden, F. W., Jr.	Listed on K CO payroll 16-22 FEB.	00/09
PVT	Evans, John. W. M.	Listed on K CO payroll 16-22 FEB. On 10 FEB, Evans, age 21, arrested for disorderly conduct and turned over to "J. Clinton Whitt" (probably 1LT White) of Company E, Fifth Regiment.	00/11
PVT	White, Charles H.	Listed on K CO payroll 16-22 FEB.	05/09
PVT	Downey, Leo J.	Enlisted 9 FEB 1904. Listed on K CO payroll 16-22 FEB.	00/00
PVT	Faber, E. A.	Listed on K CO payroll 16-22 FEB.	00/01
PVT	Faber, R. R.	Enlisted 9 FEB 1904. Listed on K CO payroll 16-22 FEB.	00/00
PVT	George, Claude	Listed on I CO payroll 16-22 FEB.	01/01
PVT	Bowersox, George W.	Enlisted 10 FEB 1904. Listed on K CO payroll 16-22 FEB.	00/00
PVT	Glessner, C. M.		00/04
PVT	Walter, William M.		03/01
PVT	Hamilton, Frank D.	Listed on K CO payroll 16-22 FEB.	00/11
PVT	Brown, H. C.	Listed on K CO payroll 16-22 FEB.	00/02
PVT	Marston, A. B.		01/02
PVT	Shipley, Charles F.	Listed on K CO payroll 16-22 FEB.	02/10
PVT	Smith, Wilbur C.		00/08
PVT	O'Brien, R. E.		00/09
PVT	Flack, G. A.		02/11
PVT	Ritter, John M.	Listed on K CO payroll 16-22 FEB.	00/09
PVT	Sparks, George W.	Listed on K CO payroll 16-22 FEB.	00/11
PVT	Niewerth, A. C.	Listed on K CO payroll 16-22 FEB.	01/04
PVT	O'Neill, John E.		04/05
PVT	Reilly, Charles E.		00/08
PVT	Gaither, L. R.		05/00
PVT	Gillaspey, C. E.		00/09
PVT	Grindall, A. J.		00/08
PVT	Hirsch, A.	Listed on K CO payroll 16-22 FEB.	00/04
PVT	Murphy, C. R.	Listed on I CO payroll 19-22 FEB.	01/01

Company F

CPT	Bowie, Washington, Jr.	Company Commander.	04/10
1LT	Conradt, Samuel E.	Company Executive Officer.	04/05
2LT	Houstoun, James P.	Total service not listed.	
1SG	Belt, T. Calvin	First Sergeant.	00/02

SGT	Danzeglock, John A.		01/09
SGT	Mahaffey, Louis H.		02/08
SGT	Murphy, William M.		01/07
SGT	Rogers, A. P.		01/05
SGT	Givan, James E.	Quartermaster Sergeant.	00/02
CPL	Griffin, John E.		00/05
CPL	Read, F. T.		02/05
CPL	Plumley, J. R.		02/05
CPL	Shelton, C. M.	Total service not listed.	
PVT	Arnold, Charles W. K.		01/01
PVT	Bailey, C. M.	Total service not listed.	
PVT	Byrne, M. J.	Total service not listed.	
PVT	Mudge, George T.		00/09
PVT	McClelland, Clifton T.	Enlisted 5 FEB 1904.	00/00
PVT	Booker, Webster		00/08
PVT	Meyer, H. F., Jr.	Enlisted 7 FEB 1904.	00/00
PVT	Cole, F. M.		00/11
PVT	Osbourn, John F.		01/04
PVT	Cantremarsh (Coutremarsh), Joseph E.	Enlisted 10 FEB 1904.	00/00
PVT	Pentz, Stanley H.	Enlisted 7 FEB 1904.	00/00
PVT	Fitchett, Y. K.		00/09
PVT	Pouder (Ponder), J. M.	Total service not listed.	
PVT	Gardner, L. W.	Total service not listed.	
PVT	Shorey, M. C.	Total service not listed.	
PVT	Hobbs, D.	Enlisted 7 FEB 1904.	00/00
PVT	Smith, William A.		00/08
PVT	Kennedy, William E. S.	On 14 FEB, Kennedy, age 21, was arrested for disobedience and intoxication while on duty. He was arrested again on 22 FEB and jailed. He was released to 1SG T. C. Belt on 23 FEB.	00/08
PVT	Taylor, E. M.	Total service not listed.	
PVT	Levonian, H.	Total service not listed.	
PVT	Thompson, A. B.	Total service not listed.	
PVT	McGuiness, J. A.		00/10
PVT	Tracey, R. J.		00/09
PVT	Boblitz, Spencer		00/08

PVT	Thomas, James	Total service not listed.	
PVT	Goodwin, Thomas H.	Enlisted 9 FEB 1904. On 12 FEB, Goodwin was arrested for disorderly conduct. He was released after paying a small fine.	00/00
PVT	Grahr, N. J.	Total service not listed.	
PVT	Hall, R. P.		00/04
PVT	Hillman, C. J.	Total service not listed.	
PVT	Lee, Edward F.		01/02
PVT	McGuiness, J. J.	Total service not listed.	
PVT	Merrifield, W. R.		01/00
PVT	Barsumian, Nazareth S.	Total service not listed.	
PVT	Davidson, J. H.		01/01
PVT	Kennedy, Edward J.	Cook. Enlisted 15 FEB 1904.	00/00
CIV	Jones, Walter	Cook. Employed 16-17 FEB.	

Company G

1LT	Heald, John R.	Company Commander.	04/05
2LT	Hancock, Frank A.	Company Executive Officer, G CO. Listed on F CO payroll 16-23 FEB.	03/00
1SG	Tinsley, Frank	First Sergeant.	23/02
SGT	Nagel, Henry		15/03
SGT	Johnson, George H.		16/01
SGT	Sindall, Robert A.		02/11
SGT	Kohlerman, John N.	Quartermaster Sergeant.	12/03
CPL	Byrne, Thomas J.	Listed on F CO payroll 16-23 FEB.	10/01
CPL	Freburger, Alex B.	Listed on F CO payroll 16-23 FEB.	05/10
CPL	Lookingland, George R.	Listed on F CO payroll 16-23 FEB.	05/09
CPL	Whitney, Wilber B.		05/09
CPL	Miller, P. Ambrose		02/01
PVT	Burke, John		01/00
PVT	Crosbie, E. A.		11/05
PVT	Eck, Harry A.	Listed on F CO payroll 16-23 FEB.	02/11
PVT	Eiser, John H.	Listed on F CO payroll 16-23 FEB.	00/09
PVT	Fitzpatrick, Thomas	Listed on F CO payroll 16-23 FEB.	11/05
PVT	Gibson, C. (E.)	Listed on F CO payroll 16-23 FEB.	00/08
PVT	Grunewald, F., Jr.	Listed on F CO payroll 16-23 FEB.	02/00
PVT	Gately, John James	Listed on F CO payroll 16-23 FEB.	00/03
PVT	Hall, George		11/05

PVT	Hewitt, Allen H.	Listed on F CO payroll 16-23 FEB.	00/08
PVT	Keene, George		00/08
PVT	Leckner, John		00/08
PVT	Minnick, George R.		00/11
PVT	Minnick, Louis N.	Listed on F CO payroll 16-23 FEB.	00/11
PVT	Newton, Samuel T.		01/01
PVT	O'Toulan, M. F.	Listed on F CO payroll 16-23 FEB.	00/08
PVT	Pitt, W. B.	Listed on F CO payroll 16-23 FEB.	00/11
PVT	Schmidt, C. E.	Listed on F CO payroll 16-23 FEB.	01/00
PVT	Pitt, R. T.		00/11
PVT	Schnur, B. A.	Listed on F CO payroll 16-23 FEB.	00/09
PVT	Taylor, E. R.		00/10
PVT	Towson, W. E.	Listed on F CO payroll 16-23 FEB.	01/01
PVT	Turner, George J.	Listed on F CO payroll 16-23 FEB.	00/08
PVT	Whitty, William	Listed on F CO payroll 16-23 FEB.	02/08
PVT	Wolfe, J. W.	Listed on F CO payroll 16-23 FEB.	00/08
PVT	Wyatt, E. L.	Listed on F CO payroll 16-23 FEB.	02/00
PVT	Wyman, S. J.	Listed on F CO payroll 16-23 FEB.	02/01
PVT	Simmons, F. R.		01/00

Company H

CPT	Holmes, E. A.	Company Commander.	11/10
1LT	Kerr, Charles G.	Company Executive Officer.	06/10
1SG	Curran, Stephen H.	First Sergeant.	04/05
SGT	Dunlop, William	Quartermaster Sergeant.	07/02
SGT	Haines, Frank H.		05/09
SGT	Chambers, William E.		02/11
SGT	Hamilton, James W.	Listed on L CO payroll 16-23 FEB.	04/05
SGT	Fewster, Joseph C.		04/05
CPL	Melvin, Chester T.		03/10
CPL	Shepherd, Percy M.		03/11
CPL	Plummer, Pinkney H.	Listed on F CO payroll 16-17 FEB.	02/04
PVT	Shannon, John T.		02/11
PVT	Smith, Charles A.		01/08
PVT	Beach, Leonard E.	Total service not listed.	
PVT	Smith, William H.		03/11
PVT	Curry, Joseph V.		02/09

PVT	Svine, Carl A.		00/07
PVT	Frazier, Samuel L.		02/07
PVT	Taylor, James, Jr.	Listed on F CO payroll 16-23 FEB.	03/09
PVT	Gerahty, Charles W.	Listed on F CO payroll 16-23 FEB.	00/07
PVT	Strohm, Thomas A., Jr.	Listed on I CO payroll 16-17 FEB.	04/08
PVT	Hartman, John	Listed on F CO payroll 16-23 FEB.	00/04
PVT	Haines, Elton R.	Listed on I CO payroll 16-22 FEB.	00/04
PVT	Lawson, William C.		02/04
PVT	Creighton, Harry	Listed on F CO payroll 16-22 FEB.	00/07
PVT	Frazier, Samuel L.	In hospital for eleven days, 12-23 FEB. Total service not listed.	
PVT	Feldhans, Harry		04/08
PVT	Price, Harry W.		01/02
PVT	Frizzell, Raymond L.	Listed on F CO payroll 17-23 FEB.	02/10
PVT	Russell, Charles I.		02/11
PVT	Bourne, Robert T.	Listed on F CO payroll 16-23 FEB.	00/06
PVT	Plummer, Edward	Listed on F CO payroll 16-23 FEB.	00/04
PVT	Rusk, Harry Welles, Jr.	Listed on F CO payroll 16-17 FEB.	01/01
PVT	Schuchart, John J.	Listed on F CO payroll 16-23 FEB.	01/01
PVT	Grothaus, David B.		00/07
PVT	Johnson, William R.	Listed on F CO payroll 16-23 FEB.	01/04
PVT	Mills, J. R.	Listed on F CO payroll 16-23 FEB.	00/07
PVT	Montell, Henry K.	Total service not listed.	
	Loistmann, Harry C.	Drummer. Total service not listed.	
	Jones, Wilmer B.	Trumpeter. Total service not listed. Listed on B CO payroll 16-23 FEB.	

Company I

CPT	Goldsborough, N. Lee	Company Commander.	36/00
1LT	Whitman, F. S.	Company Executive Officer.	08/01
2LT	Landstreet, James C.		06/00
1SG	Feldman, Albert	First Sergeant.	11/00
SGT	Iglehart, Charles		22/00
SGT	Martin, John E.		11/04
SGT	Clickner, Samuel A.	Quartermaster Sergeant 16-23 FEB.	05/10
SGT	Wickham, William H.		05/10
SGT	Hack, A. E.		03/00

CPL	Harting, L. W.		04/04
CPL	Sweeting, George		02/10
CPL	Nelson, T. T.		02/03
CPL	Orndorff, J. R.		13/10
CPL	McCruan, W. C.		01/04
PVT	Bowman, C.		01/01
PVT	Brinkley, E. H.		02/06
PVT	Brohaun, John R.		01/02
PVT	Burns, Albert		01/01
PVT	Collings, William H.		00/10
PVT	Cremer, George		00/11
PVT	Daniels, John		02/09
PVT	Davis, Howard E.		02/04
PVT	Depkin, H. D.		01/01
PVT	Depkin, F. A.		00/04
PVT	Gambrill, Daniel H.		02/10
PVT	Hahn, Albert		05/10
PVT	Hofsass, F.		02/08
PVT	Hofmann, Andrew C.		12/03
PVT	Houck, Charles		09/08
PVT	Jackson, Edwin		03/00
PVT	Jones, George L.		03/00
PVT	Vicari, S.		01/01
PVT	Webb, W. D.		01/04
PVT	Patterson, C. R.		07/01
PVT	Worley, A.		13/01
PVT	Reynolds, Lloyd William		03/00
PVT	Bonthron, Harry	Enlisted 13 FEB 1904.	00/00
PVT	Sindell, J. H.		02/00
PVT	Swithenbank, H. L.		04/11
PVT	Teano, S.		03/00
PVT	Lambie, C. B.		01/03
PVT	Poligardo, S.		07/02
PVT	Sader, John I.		02/03
PVT	Stewart, J. T., Jr.		01/02

PVT	Hundley, J. A.	Enlisted 16 FEB 1904.	00/00
PVT	Jones, George L.		03/00
PVT	Plantholt, George J.	Enlisted 18 FEB 1904.	00/00
PVT	Owens, Daniel	Enlisted 18 FEB 1904.	00/00
CIV	Passley, T.	Cook. Employed 17-22 FEB.	

Company K

CPT	Munoz, E. A.	Company Commander. Surname written with Spanish accent mark over the "n."	21/01
1LT	Daniels, Joseph N. D.	Company Executive Officer.	19/00
2LT	Hall, F. R.		09/11
1SG	Balzer, John	First Sergeant.	09/10
SGT	Arnold, Otto		09/00
SGT	McCaffray (McCaffrey), Edward		05/10
SGT	Brown, Harry M.		15/10
SGT	Porter, David D.	Listed on B CO payroll 23 FEB.	03/01
SGT	Lane, William E.	Quartermaster Sergeant.	04/09
SGT	Gascoyne, D. A.		08/10
SGT	Tonry, Albert S.		07/09
CPL	Garrett, Joseph A.		06/08
CPL	Hohman, H. S.		03/04
CPL	Pritchard, Irvin L.		04/09
CPL	Cunningham, C. H.		05/07
CPL	Austin, James H.		03/00
CPL	Wilson, W. B.		02/11
PVT	Allen, James R.		03/05
PVT	Brazel, F. J.		02/01
PVT	Brown, Howard L.		00/04
PVT	Baker, F. W.		00/09
PVT	Benning, John A.		00/02
PVT	Delahay, B. F.		00/01
PVT	Fox, A. J.		02/11
PVT	Beeler, Harry		02/10
PVT	Bernstein, Ben		01/02
PVT	Hodgedon, Ralph E.		03/04
PVT	Gerhold, Harry		00/06

PVT	Mencken, J. H.		00/02
PVT	McCauley, D. N., Jr.		00/10
PVT	Klotsch, Harry		03/10
PVT	Milton, B. J.		03/01
PVT	Liddell, Glenn		00/08
PVT	McDowell, Robert M.		03/03
PVT	Kauffman, C. A.		02/05
PVT	Katz, J. H.		00/01
PVT	Lillis, J. W.		03/04
PVT	Mills, George E.		02/10
PVT	Perkins, Boyd W.		03/11
PVT	Rupp, Walter S.		03/01
PVT	Ross, Frank B.		02/07
PVT	Webster, C. T.		02/11
PVT	Gardiner, H. E.		00/03
PVT	Klingel, Clarence		01/02
PVT	Bufelt, F. R.	Enlisted 16 FEB 1904.	00/00
PVT	Joistmann, H. C.		08/04
PVT	Kirwan, M. L.	Enlisted 16 FEB 1904.	00/00
CIV	Ogburn, Charlie	Company Cook. Employed 16-22 FEB.	

Company L

CPT	Slingluff, Jesse	Company Commander.	12/03
1LT	Brownley, W. Spear	Company Executive Officer.	14/10
2LT	Nininger, Charles M.		05/11
1SG	Thompson, Arthur	First Sergeant.	10/04
SGT	Geiglein, John G.		05/10
SGT	de Lashmutt, William R.		03/00
SGT	Gardner, William B.	Quartermaster Sergeant.	06/00
CPL	Gough, Bernard B.		04/04
CPL	Horsey, Samuel H.	Listed on I CO payroll 17-18 FEB.	02/07
CPL	Blizzard, M. H.		04/04
CPL	Sterner, H. J.		02/09
CPL	Brumbaugh, A. K.		02/01
CPL	Harrod, Howard M.	Paid $1.00/day for three days and $1.25/day for six days. Harrod wrote "PFC" (private first class) after his signature.	03/00

CPL	Hess, E. H.	Paid $1.00/day for two days and $1.25/day for fourteen days.	02/11
PVT	Adams, Harry W.		01/00
PVT	Benoit, R.		00/03
PVT	Chappelear, A. D.		02/04
PVT	Dunn, Carroll J.		01/09
PVT	Dunn, Norbert B.		01/09
PVT	Faber, Louis C.		00/02
PVT	Gill, Arthur L.		01/03
PVT	Grice, S. D.		00/08
PVT	Gross, John H.		00/11
PVT	Knight, John Milton, Jr.		00/11
PVT	Kuster, William F.		00/11
PVT	Shane, John H.		00/09
PVT	Sponheimer, Henry		00/08
PVT	Karsner, J. Walter		00/01
PVT	Stewart, Charles		00/03
PVT	Moore, Arthur L.		00/11
PVT	Vogler, Herman E., Jr.		00/08
PVT	Noakes, William		02/04
PVT	Wilson, Harry T.		00/03
PVT	Phillips, Charles H.		00/01
PVT	Walker, Percy L.		00/11
PVT	King, John F.		00/01
PVT	Mayer, Harry A.		00/08
PVT	Price, Arthur B.		00/11
PVT	Rusteberg, Charles A.		00/10
PVT	Lamar, C. Herbert		00/10
PVT	Ward, William R.		00/10
PVT	Wagner, Harry		02/04
PVT	Young, Cyrus C.		00/10
CIV	Montell, Thomas J.	Company Cook. Employed 17-23 FEB.	

Company M

CPT	Gaither, Ridgely	Company Commander.	11/05
1LT	Jenkins, David W.	Company Executive Officer. Listed on L CO payroll 22-23 FEB.	10/01
2LT	Smith, Herbert A.	Listed on K CO payroll 16-22 FEB.	05/10
1SG	Coulter, James M., Jr.	First Sergeant.	08/09
SGT	Bowie, Carlton R.	Listed on B CO payroll 16-23 FEB.	09/03
SGT	Young, Edgar K.		09/03
SGT	Winterson, John C. P.		07/05
SGT	Townsend, Charles T.		07/08
SGT	Rogers, Thornton	Quartermaster Sergeant.	03/09
CPL	Knight, James G.	Listed on B CO payroll 16-17 FEB.	05/10
CPL	Dickey, Charles E., Jr.	Listed on I CO payroll 16-22 FEB.	04/02
CPL	Hoffman, Eugene V.		07/08
CPL	Barnes, Jesse R.		04/09
CPL	Lang, Stratton M.		04/05
PVT	Adams, George I.	Listed on I CO payroll 16 FEB.	01/03
PVT	Adsit, Henry	Enlisted 11 FEB 1904.	00/00
PVT	Brundige, Thomas W., Jr.		04/09
PVT	Byrd, W. C.		02/09
PVT	Carter, B. B.	Listed on B CO payroll 16-23 FEB.	01/01
PVT	Clark, Allen, Jr.		01/08
PVT	Coners (Coner), James E.		01/01
PVT	Dickey, E. D. V.	Listed on K CO payroll 16-22 FEB.	01/01
PVT	Dinneen, J. H., Jr.	Listed on B CO payroll 16-23 FEB.	00/05
PVT	Heslop, Robert G. L.	Listed on K CO payroll 16-22 FEB.	03/04
PVT	Horn, Ernest B., Jr.		00/08
PVT	Evans, Robert William	Listed on K CO payroll 16-22 FEB.	02/04
PVT	Hughes, Thomas, Jr.	Listed on K CO payroll 16-22 FEB.	00/05
PVT	Godwin, J. E.		02/09
PVT	Johnson, Edward McK.	Listed on I CO payroll 16-22 FEB.	00/01
PVT	Handy, W. L.		03/04
PVT	Kirkness, Edward F.	Listed on B CO payroll 16-19 FEB.	05/08
PVT	Helm, W. T., Jr.	Listed on B CO payroll 16-23 FEB.	00/09
PVT	Leach, H. (Horace) H.		01/01
PVT	Dinneen, M. H.		00/05

PVT	Griffith, W. A.		00/09
PVT	Harrison, D. J.		01/03
PVT	Heslop, Frank M.	Listed on K CO payroll 16-22 FEB.	02/03
PVT	Ford, Henry, Jr.	Listed on B CO payroll 16-23 FEB.	00/08
PVT	McNair, A. C.		02/09
PVT	Mattingly, J. M.	Listed on B CO payroll 16-23 FEB.	00/08
PVT	Melvin, J. W. D.		00/08
PVT	Menshaw, Z. T.		02/04
PVT	Michel, C. H.		02/10
PVT	Wilson, Ephraim B.	Listed on B CO payroll 16-23 FEB.	00/08
PVT	Fox, S. H.	Listed on B CO payroll 18-23 FEB.	00/11
PVT	Wells, Henry S.	Listed on K CO payroll 16-22 FEB.	04/09
PVT	Vansant, Hiram D.	Listed on B CO payroll 16-20 FEB.	00/03
PVT	Packham, C. H. T.	Listed on B CO payroll 16-23 FEB.	02/01
PVT	Michel, F. G.	Listed on K CO payroll 17-22 FEB.	02/10
PVT	Slate, E. M.	Listed on K CO payroll 16-22 FEB.	00/03
PVT	Ridgely, Charles R.	Listed on B CO payroll 16-17 FEB.	02/03
PVT	Ray, Guy		01/01
PVT	Pope, G. W.	Listed on K CO payroll 16-22 FEB.	01/01
PVT	Turner, John P.	Listed on B CO payroll 16-23 FEB.	00/03
PVT	Morrison, M. L.	Listed on K CO payroll 16 FEB.	01/03

Hospital Corps

1SG	Knapp, H. C.	First Sergeant.	02/08
SGT	Hamill, G. W.		03/08
SGT	Carver, F. D.	Listed as SGT and paid $1.65/day 7-15 FEB, and as PVT $1.10/day 16-23 FEB.	03/04
SGT	Harvey, J. G., Jr.		01/09
PVT	Richardson, R. W.		01/09
PVT	Radcliffe, R. W.		01/09
PVT	Moale, John		01/04
PVT	McCarthy, Harry D.		02/03
PVT	Meyer, L. W.		00/10
PVT	Mitten, J. A.		00/02
PVT	Millikin, R. J.		01/08
PVT	Hamill, Carl W.		00/02

PVT	Smith, R. E., Jr.		00/09
PVT	Fick, Joseph G.		00/06
PVT	Scharf, C. E.		00/07
PVT	Horner, Atlie		02/02
PVT	Herman, J. G.		01/02
PVT	Gordon, Edward		01/04
PVT	Hanway, C. R.		02/07
PVT	Crook, D. C.		00/07
PVT	Byrd, Norval E.		01/00
PVT	Bryant, John Y.		02/02
PVT	Bishop, J. Z.		00/09
PVT	Blake, R. L.		01/09
PVT	Thompson, W. C.		00/07
PVT	Batchelor, James (I.)		00/08
PVT	Topscott, W.		01/04
PVT	Wisotzki, G. C.		00/03
PVT	Miller, T.		01/04
PVT	Peters, C. G.	Enlisted 4 FEB 1904.	00/00
PVT	Hoskins, A. J.		01/03
PVT	Joynes, D. J.		01/04
PVT	Jones, C. L.	Enlisted 4 FEB 1904.	00/00
PVT	Heathcote, W. E.		02/03
CIV	Brooks, Robert	Company Cook. Employed 16-20 FEB.	
CIV	Gillis, Edward	Company Cook. Employed 21-23 FEB.	

Signal Corps

1LT	Austin, Sydney B.	Commander Signal Corps.	00/04
1SG	Stewart, Joseph T.	First Sergeant.	03/00
CPL	Chaney, Waters B.	Chaney and PVT Coath directed civilian work crews that cleared overhead electric lines from the burned district.	03/00
PVT	Sweeny, H. Wilson	First Class Private.	03/00
PVT	Miller, Theodore		03/00
PVT	Coath, Clarence J.	First Class Private. Coath and CPL Chaney directed civilian work crews that cleared overhead electric lines from the burned district.	03/00
PVT	Hessler, Edward		03/00

Troop A, Cavalry

Rank	Name	Notes	Date
CPT	Shirley, Joseph W.	Executive Officer.	06/02
CPT	Hill, Charles G.	Commander Troop A.	06/02
1LT	Rogers, C. Lyon, Jr.		06/02
1SG	Rogers, James L.	First Sergeant. Elected 2LT about 18 FEB 1904.	00/02
SGT	Goodwin, W. D.		02/10
SGT	Gelston, Hugh L.		00/02
SGT	Stump, Norman		02/10
SGT	Cradock, Thomas		00/02
SGT	Shirley, H. C., Jr.		00/02
SGT	Evans, F. G.		00/02
CPL	Stimpson, H. B.		02/08
CPL	Baldwin, R. W.		02/08
CPL	Garrett, Robert	Garrett, of the prominent Garrett family, was featured in a twelve-paragraph article that appeared in the Baltimore American, 13 FEB, 1904, page 12 and in a similar article in the Baltimore News, 15 FEB, 1904, page 2.	00/02
PVT	Numsen, J. Newman		02/02
PVT	Young, J. Forney		01/11
PVT	Cockey, John C.		01/07
PVT	Sieling, H. J. W.		02/04
PVT	Sands, Frank N.		02/06
PVT	Nicholas, T. J. R.		01/06
PVT	Polk, H. R.		01/06
PVT	Naylor, Lawrence A.		01/08
PVT	Peu...inan (illegible), E. O.		01/07
PVT	Morison, H. W.		02/04
PVT	Oler, William H.		00/11
PVT	Hyde, Frank B.		00/08
PVT	Hann, Harold Curry		02/04
PVT	Wilson, Louis S.		02/08
PVT	Tregellas, S. Staley		01/11
PVT	Allen, Louis M.		00/08
PVT	Stern, T. F.		01/04
PVT	Clabaugh, A.		00/04
PVT	Neilson, G. H.		02/09

PVT	Cagle, Edwin		01/02
PVT	Keating, F. W.		01/06
PVT	Sunderland, B. B.		02/05
PVT	Nicholas, G. S.		00/07
PVT	Mullikin, H. Franklin		01/04
PVT	Hammond, Edward M.		01/09
PVT	Darnell, R. B.		01/09
PVT	Griffith, E. R.		02/02
PVT	Hill, Milton P.		00/08
PVT	Hill, D. S.		00/02
PVT	Hill, Gerald		02/07
	Jones, Edwin E.	Hospital Steward.	01/07
	Miller, C. W.	Bugler.	02/09

Naval Brigade

CDR	Geer, Edwin	Brigade Commander. Surgeon. Born: North Carolina. Geer worked in a field hospital established to treat injured firemen on 7 FEB. During Spanish-American War, Geer commanded USS Apache, USS Ajax, and was executive officer on USRS Dale.	18/00
LCR	Harrison, H. F.	Brigade Executive Officer. Cadet engineer USNA 1874-1877. During Spanish-American War, Harrison served aboard USS Katahdin and USRS Dale. Born: Maryland.	09/00
LT	Talbott, D. Russell	Surgeon. Commissioned Assistant Surgeon 17 APR 1902. Commissioned Surgeon 3 JUL 1903. Born: Maryland.	01/10
LT	Wagner, Fred H.	Chief Engineer. Commissioned LT Junior Grade 15 JAN 1902. Commissioned LT 24 MAY 1902. Born: Maryland.	02/00
LT	Putts, William E.	Commander, 2nd Division. Enlisted as seaman 26 FEB 1896. Commissioned Ensign 25 APR 1898. Served in US Navy during Spanish-American War, MAY-SEP 1898 Commissioned LT 6 FEB 1901. Born: Maryland.	03/00
LT	Willard, Edwin G.	Served in US Navy as Chief Boatswain's mate during Spanish-American War. Commissioned LT Junior Grade, 4th Division, Naval Brigade 28 DEC 1900. Commissioned LT 26 NOV 1901. Born: North Carolina.	
LT	Aspril, John	Enlisted 5 SEP 1902. Commissioned Ensign 23 MAY 1903. Commissioned LT 31 DEC 1903. Born: Delaware.	01/05
LT	Fallon, D. Robert	Paymaster. Born: Maryland.	04/07

LTJ	Reeside, John E.		Served in US Navy during the Spanish-American War, MAY-OCT 1898. Commissioned LT Junior Grade 5 APR 1900. Born: Pennsylvania.	03/10
LTJ	Gerhart (Gerhardt), William W.		Commissioned LT Junior Grade 23 NOV 1903. Born: Pennsylvania.	00/09
LTJ	Barton, J. Frederick (Fred)		Served as PVT Company H, 5th Maryland USVI 13 MAY-22 OCT 1898. Commissioned LT Junior Grade 14 NOV 1903. Lived in the Cambridge, Maryland vicinity. Born: Maryland.	
LTJ	Fallon, Charles J.		Served in US Navy as a pay clerk during Spanish-American War. Enlisted as pay yeoman 15 DEC 1897. Commissioned Ensign, 3rd Division, Naval Brigade 18 APR 1900. Commissioned LT Junior Grade 8 JAN 1901. Born: Maryland.	03/10
ENS	Page, Charles B.		Assistant Engineer. Commissioned 5 NOV 1902.	01/03
ENS	Woodruff, Charles T.		Served in Naval Brigade as a landsman, 6 SEP 1902. Commissioned Ensign 3 JUL 1903. Assigned to 5th Division, Naval Brigade 31 DEC 1903. Born: New York.	00/07
ENS	Hicks, Fessenden F.		Served in US Navy as Paymaster Clerk. Commissioned Ensign, 6th Division, 14 NOV 1903. Born: Maryland.	
ENS	Wilkinson, Pinkney W.		Captain's Aide. Commissioned Ensign 10 FEB 1904. Born: Maryland.	
ENS	Wroth, John		Served in Naval Brigade as a landsman, 1 FEB 1901. Commissioned Ensign 26 NOV 1901. Born: Maryland.	01/09
ENS	Tompkins, John A.		Assistant Surgeon. Commissioned 10 FEB 1904.	
	Niven, Edwin B.		Brigade Chaplain. Niven was reverend of the Christ Episcopal Church. Commissioned 1 NOV 1901. Born: New York.	
	Wilson		Assistant Paymaster.	

SELECT BIBLIOGRAPHY

Manuscript Collections

Maryland State Archives. ADJUTANT GENERAL (Baltimore Fire Papers) 1904 [MSA S956, MdHR 50,077-1, 2/6/5/6].

Maryland State Archives. ADJUTANT GENERAL (Baltimore Fire Papers) 1904 [MSA S956, MdHR 50,077-2, 2/8/2/22].

Maryland State Archives. ADJUTANT GENERAL (Miscellaneous Papers) February 1904 [MSA S927, MdHR 50,056-159, 2/6/4/23].

Maryland State Archives. GOVERNOR (Attorney General Opinions) 1904 [MSA S1043, MdHR 5394-1, 2/28/3/32].

Maryland State Archives. GOVERNOR (Proceedings) February 1904 [MSA S1072, MdHR 7902, 2/26/1/44].

Maryland State Archives. GOVERNOR (Reports and Investigations) 1904 [MSA S1044, MdHR 8075-5, 2/36/3/20].

Maryland State Archives. SPECIAL COLLECTIONS. (Stephen A. Goldman Collection) [MSA SC 3493-1-1, 0/66/7/27].

Maryland State Archives. TOPIC FILE (National Guard at Baltimore Fire) 1904 [MSA G 1456-1907, 0/70/9/20].

National Archives. Records of the Adjutant General's Office (Main Correspondence File, 1890-1917) RG 94. File # 518834 (add'l V), Box 3610.

Government Publications

Annual Report of the Adjutant General of Maryland, 1897.
    Baltimore: King Bros., 1898.

Annual Report of the Adjutant General of Maryland, 1900.
    Baltimore: Wm. J. C. Dulany Company, 1900.

Annual Report of the Adjutant General of Maryland, 1904-1905.
    Baltimore: King Bros., 1906.

Annual Report of the Board of Fire Commissioners for 1904.
Baltimore: Wm. J. C. Dulany Company, 1904.

Journal of Proceedings of the House of Delegates of Maryland, 1904.
Annapolis: Wm. J. C. Dulany Company, 1904.

Journal of Proceedings of the Senate of Maryland, 1904.
Annapolis: Wm. J. C. Dulany Company, 1904.

Laws of Maryland, 1896. Annapolis: Maryland General Assembly, 1896.

Law of Maryland, 1904. Annapolis: Maryland General Assembly, 1904.

Original Monthly Record of Observations.
State Weather Service, February 1904.

Report of the Board of Police Commissioners for the City of Baltimore: 1904-1905. Baltimore: Wm J. C. Dulany Company, 1906.

U.S. Bureau of the Census. *Occupations, Twelfth Census.*
Washington, DC: Government Printing Office, 1904.

Newspapers

Annapolis *Evening Capital*. February 11, 1904.

Baltimore *Afro-American Ledger*. February 13, 1904.

Baltimore *American*. February 9-24, 1904.

Baltimore *News*. February 9-13, 1904.

Baltimore *Sun*. February 9-26, 1904.

Cambridge *Democrat & News*. February 13, 1904.

Books

Callcott, Margaret Law. *The Negro in Maryland Politics 1870- 1912.*
Baltimore: Johns Hopkins Press, 1969.

Greene, Suzanne Ellery. *An Illustrated History of Baltimore*. Woodland Hills, CA: Windsor Publications, Inc., 1980.

Hann, Harold Curry. *Well Do I Remember: Memories of Old Baltimore*. Baltimore: n.p., 1953.

Kent, Frank R. *The Story of Maryland Politics*. Hatboro, PA: Traditional Press, 1968.

Meekins, George A. *Fifth Regiment, Infantry, Maryland National Guard*. Baltimore: A. Hoen & Company, 1899.

Olson, Sherry H. *Baltimore, The Building of an American City*. Baltimore: Johns Hopkins University, 1980.

Papenfuse, Edward C. and Joseph M. Coale, III. *Atlas of Historical Maps of Maryland, 1608-1908*. Baltimore: Johns Hopkins University Press, 1982.

Riley, Elihu S. *A History of the General Assembly of Maryland 1635-1904*. Baltimore: Nunn & Company, 1905.

Rosen, Christine Meisner. *The Limits of Power, Great Fires and The Process of City Growth in America*. New York: Cambridge University Press, 1986.

White, Frank F. Jr. *The Governors of Maryland 1777-1970*. Annapolis: Hall of Records Commission, 1970.

Williams, Harold A. *Baltimore Afire*. Baltimore: Schneidereith & Sons, 1954.

Name Index

A

Abicht, Robert 69
Ackerman, John 54
Adams, C. J. 57
Adams, Charles W. 41
Adams, Frank H. 57
Adams, George I. 88
Adams, Harry W. 87
Adams, Sebastion H. 38
Adkins, Charles E. 46
Adkins, Joda 46
Adsit, Henry 88
Agnew, William J. 44
Ahring, W. 68
Aidt, Louis 70
Airey, Ernest 38
Alexander, William W. 75
Allard, C. G. 77
Allen, Edward 62
Allen, Frank 68
Allen, James H. 61
Allen, James R. 85
Allen, Louis M. 91
Allen, Thomas 54
Allen, Thomas S. 69
Allen, William G. 71
Allerton, S. M. 51
Allnutt, George B. 47
Alsip, Charles M. 36
Alvey, Charles 34
Alvey, H. C. 34
Anacker, Herman F. 57
Anacker, William 56
Anderson, H. W. 72
Anderson, James 37
Andrews, Roland 37
Andrews, William B. 67
Applegarth, William 70
Archer, J. Glasgow 39
Archer, R. Harris, Jr. 39
Arminger, Henry J. 63
Arminger, Sidney 70
Armstrong, William E. 59
Arney, E. H. 55
Arnold, Calvin W. 62
Arnold, Charles W. K. 80
Arnold, Edward S. 65
Arnold, Lyman M. 44
Arnold, Otto 85
Arring, James W. 64
Ash, Joshua M. 40

Ashbury, Howard E. 72
Askey, William M. 64
Aspril, John 92
Assner, Allen 62
Atkinson, M. S., Jr. 73
Atkinson, Warren 65
Austin, James H. 85
Austin, Sydney B. 25, 90
Ayers, Charles H., Jr. 40
Ayers, James A. 64
Ayers, Warren C. 49

B

Baerwald, Richard E. 63
Baetzer, Charles H. 72
Bagon, W. J. 51
Bailey, C. M. 80
Bailey, William C. 48
Baker, Albert 36
Baker, Alonzo P. 39
Baker, F. W. 85
Baker, Oliver L. 37
Baldwin, R. W. 91
Ball, Joseph 41
Balzer, John 85
Banks (Barry), Albert 64
Barber, Joseph H. 36
Bareford, J. T. 75
Barkley, Jesse 37
Barncord, Jerry 36
Barnes, Charles F. 44
Barnes, Clarence 44
Barnes, Howard J. 44
Barnes, Jesse R. 88
Barnes, John 60
Barrett, Henry S. 33
Barrett, Samuel G. 65
Barsumian, Nazareth S. 81
Barton, J. Frederick (Fred) 93
Bast, Alfred 62
Batchelor, James (I.) 90
Bauer, C. A. 74
Bauge, George 59
Baxter, William 60
Baylor, Robert M. 35
Beach, Charles 52
Beach, Leonard E. 82
Beadenkoff, William P. 58
Beale, James 53
Beale, L. 58
Beale, S. J. 52

Beall, Benjamin Lloyd 53
Beall, Harry L. 49
Beall, James H. V. 42
Beall, William V. 49
Bean, Harry E. 49
Beard, Spencer 47
Beatty, Henry C. 56
Bechtel, G. K. 75
Bechtel, R. H. 75
Becker, I. 34
Beckett, Thomas M. O. 64
Beeler, Harry 85
Bell, C. K. 51
Bell, Edward F. 72
Bell, G. W. 51
Bell, Samuel K. 64
Bell, W. A. 77
Belt, T. Calvin 79
Bennett, Anthony W. 56
Bennett, Charles E. 46
Bennett, Edwin J. 64
Bennett, Joseph 60
Benning, John A. 85
Benoit, R. 87
Benson, Charles M. 78
Benson, T. B. 47
Bentz, Joseph W. 44
Bereford, J. T. 77
Bernstein, Ben 85
Berry, R. B. 74
Bevan, William F. 73
Binau, A. 51
Binnix, C. W. 54
Birkholz, Harry 69
Bishop, J. Z. 90
Bishop, John T. 75
Bitz, F. 51
Bitzel, Philip W. 44
Bixby, Harry M. 61
Bladin, C. E. 77
Blair, William H. 77
Blake, Herbert C. 62
Blake, R. L. 90
Blank, L. N. 51
Blizzard, M. H. 86
Block, Harry 70
Bloom, Isaac 65
Blum, Frank 75
Boblitz, Spencer 80
Bohlman, Henry 62
Bohlmann, Henry 67
Bollinger, Scott C. 44
Bond, A. 53
Bond, Oliver 53

Bonthron, Harry 84
Booker, Webster 80
Bookman, Gust 61
Bora, Antony (Toni) 68
Bora, Fillip 69
Bornscheuer, John 78
Bornsheuer, Adolph 78
Bosely, James 10
Bottorf, Benjaman F. 57
Bourke, Benjamin F. 49
Bourne, Robert T. 83
Boush, James C. 49
Bowen, Howard W. 78
Bowen, James H. 75
Bowers, Charles H. 36
Bowers, Howell B. 42
Bowersox, A. E. 77
Bowersox, George W. 79
Bowie, Carlton R. 88
Bowie, Robert B. 72
Bowie, Washington, Jr. 4, 79
Bowman, C. 84
Boyce, A. P. 73
Boyd, Charles 70
Bozman, James 46
Brackett, James F. (Frank) 49
Brady, Upton S. 24, 72
Brannock, Charles 38
Bray, Edmund H. 34
Brazel, F. J. 85
Brenaman, H. L. 35
Brent, Edward 59
Brent, John P. 54
Brenton, Wallace C. 59
Brewer, Charles E. 61
Brewer, Charles W. 61
Brewer, Lloyd 47
Brewer, Nicholas 46
Brewer, William R. 46
Brewington, W. K. 46
Brinkley, E. H. 84
Briscoe, F. B. 68
Brohaun, John R. 84
Brooks, Robert 69, 90
Brounel, J. Wallace 38
Brown, C. P. 67
Brown, Edward H. 45
Brown, H. C. 79
Brown, Harry M. 85
Brown, Howard 49
Brown, Howard L. 85
Brown, J. L. 77
Brown, John W. 45
Brown, Richard 53

Brown, William B. 51
Brown, William E. 60
Browne, H. A. 73
Brownley, W. Spear 24, 86
Bruce, James G. 65
Brumbaugh, A. K. 86
Brundige, Thomas W., Jr. 88
Brushweller, William J. 61
Bryan, Carryl H. 72
Bryan, James W. 36
Bryan, Raymond C. 48
Bryan, William S. Jr. 27
Bryant, John Y. 90
Buchanan, Thomas G. 72
Buckey, William 35
Bucklen, E. R. 51
Bufelt, F. R. 86
Buffington, A. G. 53
Bufter, W. S. 55
Bull, Oscar 56
Bundy, C. S. 75
Burck, William A. 50
Burgess, William H., Jr. 57
Burke, E. 51
Burke, Harry W. 64
Burke, John 81
Burkhead, William 67
Burness, J. M. 52
Burneston, William N. 64
Burnett, H. C. 59
Burns, Albert 84
Burns, Edward J. 53
Burns, Milton R. 64
Burr, Edward 28
Burton, Clifton 54
Burton, Guy 56
Burus, Milton R. 64
Busch, Cornelius 61
Bussell, John M. 64
Butler, Albert 57
Butler, James 37
Butler, William P. 39
Byrd, Norval E. 90
Byrd, W. C. 88
Byrne, M. J. 80
Byrne, Thomas J. 81
Byrnes, W. A. 77

C

Cadell, Samuel J. 68
Cadwell, Charles C. 33
Cagle, Edwin 92
Callahan, Thomas D. 72
Calwel, George 67
Cameron, Andrew 40
Campbell, William E. 42
Cantremarsh (Coutremarsh), Joseph E. 80
Carey, French S. 25 - 26
Carpenter, C. S. 35
Carr, D. J. 47
Carr, H. S. 47
Carr, John R. 68
Carr, William B. 46
Carre, Clarence 70
Carroll, A. F. 70
Carroll, Charles W. 43
Carroll, James R. 38
Carroll, Joseph 54
Carroll, Wallace 42
Carter, B. B. 88
Carter, Charles W. 63
Carver, F. D. 89
Cary, French S. 60
Casey, James C. 34
Cassell, William H. 57
Catheart, H. G. 74
Caulbourn, L. P. 45
Cavalien, L. H. 55
Chambers, George 68
Chambers, James M. 61
Chambers, William E. 82
Chance, Willie Julian 48
Chaney, Waters B. 90
Chappelear, A. D. 87
Chappell, John E. 42
Charlton, W. 60
Chatham, James S. 45
Childs, George 75
Chinn, E. Lacy 49
Christopher, T. J. 55
Clabaugh, A. 91
Clark, Allen, Jr. 88
Clark, Charles L. 56
Clark, George 37
Clark, Isaac N. 40
Clark, Lawrence 61
Clark, Robert S. 40
Clark, Thaddeus W. 71
Clark, Thomas A. 35
Clark, William H. 37
Clathey, James M. 54
Claude, W. C. 34
Claypoole, William 75
Clazey, William 56
Clickner, Samuel A. 83
Clotworthy, C. Baker 71
Coale, F. W. 33

Coale, R. Dorsey 72
Coath, Clarence J. 90
Cockey, John C. 91
Cockey, W. B. 33
Cockrill, H. C. 77
Colbourn (Calbourn), George 38
Colder, Albert F. 38
Colder, E. Hall 38
Colder, George C. 39
Cole, F. M. 80
Cole, Frank 67
Cole, George E. 60
Cole, John Herbert 42
Coligi, Raffala (Raphael) 69
Collings, William H. 84
Collins, Charles 42
Collins, James Thomas 37
Collins, John 47
Collins, John L. 46
Collins, John P. 43
Collison, John W. 42
Collison, Walter T. 42
Collison, William 41
Combs, James 58
Compton, Arch 57
Conaway, William 66
Coners (Coner), James E. 88
Connelly, S. B. 47
Connor, Albert R. 70
Conrad, Schick 62
Conradt, S. E. 4, 24
Conradt, Samuel E. 79
Constable, William P. 40
Cook, R. R. 77
Cooke, F. D. 75
Cooper, Arthur M. 62
Cooper, C. 68
Cooper, C. V. M. 78
Cornell, Eugene M. 49
Corridean, Joseph 40
Cottrill, Leo D. 36
Coulbourn, L. P. 26
Coulter, James M., Jr. 88
Councill (Council), Willie 48
Councill, Frank 48
Cox, Harry E. 49
Cox, Joseph Harry 42
Cradock, Thomas 91
Craggs, R. 77
Cranford, Ralph R. 50
Crauford (Cranford), Zachariah S. 49
Crawford, A. 67
Creighton, Harry 83
Cremer, George 84

Crook, D. C. 90
Crooks, J. Irvin 53
Crosbie, E. A. 81
Crosby, Thomas J. 43
Crumberker (Crumbacker), Arthur 44
Cumberland, William 71
Cunningham, C. H. 85
Curran, Stephen H. 82
Curry, C. E. 55
Curry, Joseph V. 82
Cushing, W. W. 73
Czarnowsky, Herbert (F.) 72

D

Dailey, H. 58
Daly, Henry T. 74
Dame, W. M. 71
Daniels, Charles S. (L.) 40
Daniels, John 84
Daniels, Joseph N. D. 85
Danzeglock, John A. 80
Darnell, R. B. 92
Darr, J. William 59
Daumman, H. S. 51
Davey, Raymond O. J. 50
Davidson, J. H. 81
Davies, John H. 36
Davies, Rowland J. 36
Davis, Charles 53
Davis, Claude G. 48
Davis, Daniel 49
Davis, George 69
Davis, Howard E. 84
Davis, S. G., Jr. 71
Davis, Thomas H. 48
Davis, Warner 57
Davis, William 71
Dawes, Joseph B. 35
Dawson, Edward W. 65
Day, Edward 47
Day, Thomas J. 78
de Guise, Carroll 78
de Lashmutt, William R. 86
Dean, James N. 38
DeBaufre, Berry 62
DeBon, Leon 39
Debring, Walter R. 63
Degel, Charles 58
Degel, Henry 58
Delahay, B. F. 85
Dell, Russell F. 45
Dell, Winter C. 44
Denmead, Arthur R. 76
Dennis, H. 52

Denver, W. Frank 43
Depkin, F. A. 84
Depkin, H. D. 84
Derr, F. L. 74
Derreth, J. 51
Devine, Edward J. 68
Dickey, Charles E., Jr. 88
Dickey, E. D. V. 88
Diffenderfer, C. R. 72
Dinneen, J. H., Jr. 88
Dinneen, M. H. 88
Disharoon, Lein (Levin) 45
Dixon, A. P. 35
Dixon, Ira 63
Dodson, Harry 54
Dogge, Albert H. 72
Doggett, William H. 39
Donahue, E. J. 68
Donahue, J. A. 77
Donnelly, F. B. 54
Donnelly, James E. 65
Donohue, J. W. 59
Dooley, W. J. 76
Dooling, Percy 41
Dorn, George 60
Dorr, Joseph 70
Dorris, John B. W. 35
Dorsey, William 53
Doster, C. 58
Dougherty, B. 77
Douglass, Samuel R. 45
Downey, J. W. 34
Downey, Leo J. 79
Downing, Cannon J. 46
Downs, D. 56
Doyle, Samuel M. 41
Drexel, Robert 59
Drexel, Walter 59
Dryden, F. W., Jr. 79
Duce, Charles K. 26, 63
Duer, Harry Lay 73
Dukehart, G. J. 74
Dukehart, H. P. 74
Dukehart, J. A. B. 73
Dukehart, J. Krebs 73
Dukehart, M. J. 74
Dunker, Harry J. 70
Dunlap, James R. 34
Dunlop, William 82
Dunn, Carroll J. 87
Dunn, Norbert B. 87
Dunn, Richard 38
Dunn, W. 38
Durben, Roy John 44

Duval, E. B. 72
Duvall, Charles S. 70
Duvall, W. P. 73
Dwyer, Paul P. 74

E

Eason, Norman A. 42
Eaton, G. 56
Ebling, William 49
Eck, Charles 51
Eck, Harry A. 81
Eckenrode, Joseph G. 45
Eckstein, Albert 74
Edell, D. J. 76
Eisel, Fred 58
Eisenhart, John W. 44
Eiser, John H. 81
Eliason, C. 67
Emerich, William V. 64
Emery, Oliver 64
Emge 67
Emrich, George 47
Englar, Frank, Jr. 45
Engleman, David J. 44
Enos, C. O. 35
Erb, Carl 44
Erler, George R. 77
Ernst, F. J. 75
Ernst, William F. 75
Eurice (Eurich), George 63
Evans, F. G. 91
Evans, John. W. M. 79
Evans, Robert William 88
Everhart, George Y. 16

F

Faber, E. A. 79
Faber, Louis C. 87
Faber, R. R. 79
Fairbanks, Wilbur 58
Falk, Paul 76
Fallon, Charles J. 93
Fallon, D. Robert 92
Farlow, Charles 46
Farlow, Harvey G. 46
Farmer, James G. 35
Farnan, Thomas F. 3
Faulkner, James O. 48
Favorite, Edward T. 36
Favour, John G. 39
Feaga, H. C. 35
Feldhans, Harry 83
Feldman, Albert 83
Feldpusch, Ferdinand 75

Fendley, John W., Jr. 66
Ferguson, Thomas 42
Ferguson, William A. 41
Fewster, Joseph C. 82
Fick, Joseph G. 90
Filbert, Samuel W. 70
Finnan, Cletus 40
Finney, J. M. T. 33
Firsch, H. E. 54
Fischer, J. F. Albert 64
Fish, R. S. 47
Fisher, B. F. 74
Fisher, Charles E. 45
Fisher, George L. 36
Fisher, H. E. 55
Fisher, James Ray (Roy) 37
Fisher, John H. 43
Fisher, Winfield 75
Fitchett, Y. K. 80
Fitz, E. L. 60
Fitzpatrick, Thomas 81
Flack, G. A. 79
Flemming, Archibald J. 45
Flowers, Harry 39
Flowers, Holton H. 48
Flowers, Warren 39
Foble, John B. 38
Ford, Henry, Jr. 89
Foreacre, George G. 40
Foreman, A. E. 77
Foreman, Custer B. 78
Forsyth, Christ 37
Fort, S. J. 33
Forvitz, Harry J. 69
Fowler, Charles F. (T.) 45
Fowler, Charles W. 69
Fowler, Fred 55
Fowler, George 59
Fowler, John D. 45
Fowler, John J. 67
Fox, A. J. 85
Fox, G. F. 76
Fox, Jacob 61
Fox, S. H. 89
Frank, George 68
Frazier, Samuel L. 83
Freberger, Caswell B. 69
Freburger, Alex B. 81
Freeman, D. S. 73
Freeman, Joseph P. 42
Freeman, William H. (Ed) 66
Frey, William W. B. 77
Frittita, Joseph 68
Frizzell, Raymond L. 83

Frizzell, William E. 44
Frush (Fresh), Walter H. 36

G

Gaither, Bernard 50
Gaither, Charles D. 27, 33
Gaither, E. H. 26
Gaither, Ernest H. 60
Gaither, H. W., Jr. 73
Gaither, L. R. 79
Gaither, Ridgely 88
Gambrill, Daniel H. 84
Gardiner, George A. 42
Gardiner, H. E. 86
Gardner, H. K. 52
Gardner, L. W. 80
Gardner, William B. 86
Garrett, Joseph A. 85
Garrett, Robert 28, 91
Garrett, William T. 52
Gascoyne, D. A. 85
Gately, John James 81
Gates, John L. 49
Gaylord (Gayland), J. Clinton 54
Geer, Edwin 92
Geiglein, John G. 86
Geist, Walter S. 52
Gelston, Hugh L. 91
George, Barry 74
George, C. H. 57
George, Claude 79
George, Howard 59
George, John 38
George, Stephen H. 59
Georges, Joseph M. 59
Geraci, Frank B. 42
Geraci, Joseph T. 34
Gerahty, Charles W. 83
Gerhart (Gerhardt), William W. 93
Gerhold, Harry 85
Gewecke, Charles H. 76
Gibson, C. (E.) 81
Gibson, George G. 65
Gibson, William H. 69
Gill, Albert S. 25, 59
Gill, Arthur L. 87
Gillaspey, C. E. 79
Gillesful, William 61
Gillespie, James T., Jr. 65
Gillespie, William 64
Gilley, George 61
Gilley, Martin 61
Gillis, C. Lee 46
Gillis, Edward 90

Girvin, John N. 39
Givan, James E. 80
Gladstone, Charles 60
Gladstone, William 63
Glanding, W. L. 54
Glascott, H. C. 47
Glessner, C. M. 79
Glocker, Albert E. 72
Godwin, J. E. 88
Golden, David 69
Golden, Joseph 61
Goldsborough, James P. 48
Goldsborough, N. Lee 83
Good, Herbert J. 37
Goodrich (Goodrick), E. M. 75
Goodwin, Thomas H. 81
Goodwin, W. D. 91
Gootee, Brice B. 63
Gootee, Bruce B. 3, 23 - 24, 26
Gordon, Edward 90
Gorman, Arthur Pue 17, 27
Gorman, B. J. 72
Gormley, H. B. 55
Goslyn, Charles (Charley) 38
Gosnell, John T. 74
Goss, L. V. 61
Gossard, Martin L. 36
Goudy, N. A. 51
Gough, Bernard B. 86
Gould, D. U. 52
Grace, Philip G. 41
Graham, Charles E. 35
Grahr, N. J. 81
Green, Bernard 65
Green, Edward 78
Greene, Allie 47
Greene, W. 55
Greenhawk, Frank A. 41
Greenhood, L. 67
Greenhood, T. 55
Greves, David W. 76
Grice, S. D. 87
Grier, Fred A., Jr. 45
Griffin, B. 53
Griffin, John E. 80
Griffith, Carroll S. 74
Griffith, E. R. 92
Griffith, J. Milton 33
Griffith, W. A. 89
Grimes, William Taylor 45
Grindall, A. J. 79
Gross, John H. 87
Grothaus, David B. 83
Grove, Melchor C. 36

Groverman, Arthur 59
Grunewald, F., Jr. 81
Gruss, Fred A. 72
Gunther, Chriss 49

H

Hack, A. E. 83
Hager, Richard 36
Hahn, Albert 84
Hahn, Charles 51
Haines, Elton R. 83
Haines, Frank H. 82
Haines, W. J. 34
Hall, Edward J. 68
Hall, F. R. 85
Hall, George 81
Hall, R. P. 81
Hall, S. G. 76
Hall, Thomas W. 39
Hall, Walter C. 69
Hally, Albert L. 35
Hamberry, M. J. 60
Hamill, Carl W. 89
Hamill, G. W. 89
Hamilton, Frank D. 79
Hamilton, James W. 82
Hamilton, S. 52
Hamilton, Samuel 69
Hamley, L. E. 78
Hammon, F. 58
Hammond, Charles P. 41
Hammond, Edward M. 92
Hammond, Hiram P. 46
Hammond, James Edward 52
Hancock, Frank A. 81
Handy, W. L. 88
Haney, Walter J. 66
Hann, Harold Curry 29, 91
Hann, John R. 44
Hanna, James C. 38
Hanson, W. Ward 74
Hanson, Walter S. 60
Hanway, C. R. 90
Hardcastle, Robert 41
Hardesty, James M. 65
Harding, R. M. 55
Hardy, John 59
Hargrove, William 58
Harrison, D. J. 89
Harrison, H. F. 92
Harrod, Howard M. 86
Harting, L. W. 84
Hartman, H. M. 51
Hartman, John 83

103

Hartzel, W. J. 58
Hartzell, Milton E. 71
Harvey, J. G., Jr. 89
Harward, J. Wilson 39
Hasselberg, Fred 70
Hassett, T. H. (Howard) 38
Hastings, A. 58
Haukin, William 54
Haupt, G. F. 54
Haupt, George F. 23, 28
Haupt, James H. 53
Hauser, William 68
Hayden, Alfred C. 48
Hayden, Clarence 57
Hayden, Edward G. 48
Hayden, Lloyd T. 48
Hayes, J. S. 57
Hayes, John T. 60
Hayman, Sewell P. 45
Haynes, Harry E. 66
Heald, John R. 81
Healey, William J. 65
Heathcote, W. E. 90
Heineman, August 62
Heinemann, A. A. 55
Heird, Howell H. 45
Helfrich, Anthony C. 57
Hellen, Charles 70
Heller, F. 55
Helm, W. T., Jr. 88
Henkelmann, Edward 65
Henry, Adkins 73
Henry, Harry E. 38
Hepburn, George L. 58
Herbert, Orril 47
Herkorn, William H. 57
Herman, J. G. 90
Herring, Joseph T. 34
Heslop, Frank M. 89
Heslop, Robert G. L. 88
Hess, E. H. 87
Hessler, Edward 90
Hessler, Emil Edward 60
Hevie, W. 77
Hewitt, Allen H. 82
Hickman, C. D. 51
Hickman, Harry S. 57
Hickman, Herbert D. 66
Hicks, Fessenden F. 93
Higgenbothom (Higgenbottom), Charles H. 66
Higgins, J. J., Jr. 47
Hildebrandt, Charles H. 53
Hill, Charles G. 91

Hill, Charles Irving 50
Hill, D. S. 92
Hill, Gerald 92
Hill, Milton P. 92
Hill, William H. 69
Hillman, C. J. 81
Hillman, E. W. 45
Hillman, Harry 62
Hiltner, Harry 62
Hiltner, John F. 57
Hilton, John E. 46
Hilton, William B. 36
Hines, James W. 66
Hinkey, John 5
Hinkley, John 5 - 6, 24, 71
Hinton, George L. 50
Hirkomer (Hirkorm), William H. 69
Hirsch, A. 79
Hirt, Adolph 37
Hirt, William 63
Hirth, Daniel 78
Hitchner, J. Gorman 40
Hitchner, John G. 40
Hobbs, D. 80
Hobbs, James C. 76
Hobbs, Osborn 66
Hodeck, Joseph 53
Hodgedon, Ralph E. 85
Hoefer (Hofer), Walter 68
Hoeflich, G. W. 55
Hoffman, C. 68
Hoffman, Edmund H. 56
Hoffman, Eugene V. 88
Hoffman, John M. 58
Hoffman, William 68
Hofmann, Andrew C. 84
Hofsass, F. 84
Hoge, Otto H. 38
Hoge, William F. 37
Hohman, H. S. 85
Holden, James H. 48
Holidayoke, D. F. 34
Holidayoke, William E. 49
Hollan, J. 67
Holland, Fred 43
Holland, George F. 61
Holland, John Leo 66
Holliday, Henry, Jr. 34
Hollingsworth, D. F. (Richard) 39
Hollingsworth, R. J. 73
Holmes, Charles F. 40
Holmes, E. A. 82
Holmes, Presley H. 44
Holmes, W. Pinkney 3, 23, 25, 29, 71

Holt, E. W. 46
Holt, S. E. 46
Holton, Charles A. 43
Holtz, H. 69
Homer, Charles C. 17, 27
Hopkins, Edgar E. 42
Hopkins, T. Kenton 39
Hopper, C. D. 76
Horan, James 61
Horn, Ernest B., Jr. 88
Horner, Atlie 90
Horsey, Samuel H. 86
Horton, George W. 2, 23
Hose, John S. 37
Hoskins, A. J. 90
Houck, Charles 84
Houstoun, James P. 24, 79
Howard, Harvey 49
Howard, Oliver E. 50
Howard, Willard 50
Howser, Charles H. (Harry) 48
Hoy, W. 55
Hubbard, William 43
Hubley, Clyde W. 59
Hudgins, Charles J. 64
Hudgins, George 58
Hudson, John 46
Hughes, Thomas, Jr. 88
Hull, Samuel W. 64
Hultz, Harry 56
Hummel, Charles E. 66
Hummel, George E. 57
Humphreys, G. R. 46
Humphreys, Louis 46
Hundley, J. A. 85
Hurst, J. Howard 37
Hurt, W. 56
Hutchins, S. J. 68
Hutton, H. M. 71
Hyde, Benjamin 43
Hyde, Daniel 43
Hyde, Frank B. 91
Hyman, Clarence E. 76

I

Iglehart, Charles 83
Illig, Charles O. 62
Ironmonger, Charles H. 59
Isaac, Gilbert 56
Iseralson, Michel 69
Ivey, James 43

J

Jackson, Edwin 84
Jacobs, Arthur G. 43
Jacobs, John R. 66
Jacobson, John 57 - 58
Jacobson, Walter S. 58
Jandorf, M. F. 55
Janney, Thomas S. 24, 74
Jefferson, A. 60
Jenkins, C. F. 67
Jenkins, Charles R. 73
Jenkins, David W. 88
Jenkins, Robert E. 62
Jenkins, W. (Q.) 73
Jester, Washington 48
Jewell, H. J. 34
Johns, W. J. 52
Johnson, Alan D. 40
Johnson, E. C. 71
Johnson, Edward McK. 88
Johnson, George 68
Johnson, George D. 72
Johnson, George H. 81
Johnson, Harry M. 49
Johnson, J. Roy 46
Johnson, Walter A. 16 - 17, 27
Johnson, William R. 83
Johnston, Wilson 61
Joistmann, H. C. 86
Jones, A. B. 52
Jones, A. W. 53, 60
Jones, Albert 36
Jones, C. L. 90
Jones, Edward J. 42
Jones, Edward W. 41
Jones, Edwin E. 92
Jones, Frank H. 75
Jones, George 59
Jones, George L. 84 - 85
Jones, Harry C. 24, 50
Jones, Harry, C. 4
Jones, Harvey L. 19, 28, 62
Jones, J. Radcliffe, Jr. 37
Jones, Lewis M. 36
Jones, N. L. 54
Jones, Oliver 71
Jones, Spencer Cone 16
Jones, Walter 81
Jones, Wilmer B. 83
Joyce, T. 55
Joynes, D. J. 90
Jump, C. H. 77

K

Kachner, J. F.   75
Kaesemeyer, George W.   72
Kamphaus, August   75
Kane, James F.   65
Kane, Oscar   63
Kansler, William H.   76
Karcher, Alfred G.   65
Karl, Felix   78
Karsner, J. Walter   87
Kasemeyer, George W.   34
Katz, J. H.   86
Kauffman, C. A.   86
Kearney, J.   56
Keating, B. P., Jr.   73
Keating, F. W.   92
Keen, Walter K.   38
Keenan, Frank   56
Keene, George   82
Kelchner, G. A. M.   46
Kelley, John H.   50
Kelly, James   66
Kelly, John (T.)   40
Kelly, Thomas F.   64
Kelly, William   63
Kelly, William L.   76
Kennedy, Edward J.   81
Kennedy, Harry   35
Kennedy, William E. S.   80
Kerchner, F. W.   77
Kermet, Fred O.   71
Kernan, Charles L.   57
Kerr, Charles G.   82
Kessler, C.   52
Keyes, J. Clifton   23, 57
Keys, Herbert   56
Keyser, Henry B.   71
Killmeyer, Fred   60
Killmeyer, Robert M.   59
King, John   67
King, John F.   87
Kingsbury, L. L.   51
Kingsbury, Lester   24
Kirby, Thomas   48
Kirkness, Edward F.   88
Kirkwood, Thomas   73
Kirwan, M. L.   86
Kisling, Norman L.   38
Kisling, Willie S.   38
Klakring, Leslie   50
Klimm, George   75
Klingel, Clarence   86
Klingmeyer, H. W.   55
Klotsch, Harry   86
Knapp, H. C.   89
Knapp, William G.   59
Knauff (Knauft), William H.   63
Knauff, Joseph   66
Kneisley, Herbert L.   34
Knell, Joseph K.   71
Knight, James G.   88
Knight, John Milton, Jr.   87
Knight, William C.   61
Knoche, Frank   74
Knode, Alfred   36
Knoerr, Jacob   75
Knofler, Melvin C.   39
Koch, John S.   42
Koerner (Koener), Edward   61
Koerner, Henry   61
Kohl, John J.   76
Kohler, Harry C.   58
Kohlerman, John N.   81
Kone, Walter H.   56
Kramer, Charles H., Jr.   64
Kraskell, J. H.   53
Krastell, Joseph   59
Krause, Rudolph E.   61
Krauss, Perry   52
Krauss, S.   51
Krentzer, C. R.   74
Kretzer, Henry   36
Kriechbaum, George   63
Krieg, Charles   74
Krug, Henry G.   64
Kurt, William   53
Kuster, William F.   87
Kuts (Keets), Edward   47

L

Laib, F. K.   74
Lamar, C. Herbert   87
Lamar, Marion (Bruce)   36
Lamb, C. G.   34
Lambert, Arthur   65
Lambie, C. B.   84
Landstreet, James C.   83
Lane, Thomas Roy   48
Lane, William E.   85
Lang, Stratton M.   88
Lang, William   40
Langford, C. A.   75
Laroque, J. M.   74
Latham, Clarence   37
Latimer, Thomas E.   37
Lauke, Frederick   62
Lawrence, Harry C.   74

Lawson, William C. 83
Lawyer, William G. (Grove) 43
Layton, Arthur C. (Charles A.) 66
Le Tournan, Harry 49
Leach (Leech), William 61
Leach, H. (Horace) H. 88
League, Eugene O. 50
League, H. M. 55
Leckner, John 82
LeCompte, William A. F. 62
Lednum, Jesse A. 41
Lee, Charles A. 70
Lee, Clarence 53
Lee, Edward F. 81
Leffert, William E. 45
Legg, Charles E. 63
Leimbach, George C. 56
Leister, Guy W. 45
Lemkes, H. (Hamond) 66
Levering, F. A., Jr. 73
Levering, H. Brooke 73
Levonian, H. 80
Lewis, D. C. 53, 68
Lewis, H. C. 56
Lewis, Harry 62
Lewis, Herbert 40
Lewis, R. W. 52
Liddell, Glenn 86
Lillis, J. W. 86
Lingerman, Louis 67
Linke, John H. 64
Linson, K. L. 52
Lipsch, Max 63
List, George S. 61
List, Milton 61
List, Oscar C. 57
List, S. E. 74
Little, Charles A. 34
Little, Clarence J. 60
Litz, George 62
Livingston, George A. 78
Livingston, Harry C. 77
Livingston, J. R. P., Jr. 46
Lloyd, Daugherty 69
Loane, J. D. 51
Loane, Joseph 59
Lockwood, Frank 76
Loistmann, Harry C. 83
Long, C. Arthur 76
Long, W. T. 52
Lookingland, George R. 81
Loomis, Charles L. 51
Lottes, Louis 72
Louck, F. 25

Love, Harry 42
Loveday, William N. 41
Lowery, Joseph 67
Lowman, John R. 43
Lowndes, Charles H. G. 73
Lowry, John 66
Lucas, H. 71
Lucas, Joseph S. 63
Lunder (Lender), Charles 69
Lutz, Walter 67
Lyman, Albert E. 70
Lyon, C. L. 54
Lyon, J. W., Jr. 73
Lyons, J. W. 52

M

MacCalman, Duncan 50
Mace, Jesse 50
Mace, Laurence 53
Macklin, C. F. 33
MacNeal, Fred R. 40
Magereth, Henry H. 63
Magness, John 64
Magruder, Edward K. 35
Mahaffey, Louis H. 80
Mahoney, Harry E. 40
Mahoney, J. Thomas 40
Mahoney, William J. 40
Malone, T. Henry 38
Manger, Faryl C. (Joseph) 45
Mangold, William 76
Manner, William 38
Manning, John P. 45
Markel, William 71
Markoe, John S. 77
Marley, John 61, 70
Marshall, Harry 59
Marshall, Horace 50
Marshall, J. C. 34
Marston, A. B. 79
Martin, John E. 83
Martin, Robert C. 66
Marye, R. Turner 73
Mason, Steven Thomson 73
Mattingly, J. M. 89
Mayer, Harry A. 87
Mayers, Charles 68
Maykrantz, Albert 58
Mayo, George B. 43
McAllister, Frank 66
McAllister, Joseph V. 35
McCabe, James 71
McCaffray (McCaffrey), Edward 85
McCann, John H. 43

McCarthy, C. D.   55
McCarthy, Harry D.   89
McCarthy, W. J.   55
McCauley, D. N., Jr.   86
McCauley, J. Hayes   40
McCaull, J. A.   67
McCeney, Jacob   70
McClean, Charles B.   34
McClelland, Clifton T.   80
McCollough, Edward   47
McComas, J. L.   52
McComas, Walter R.   38
McCruan, W. C.   84
McCurley, James B.   65
McCurley, William   66
McDonald, Edward   76
McDonald, James   40
McDowell, Robert M.   86
McGuiness, J. A.   80
McGuiness, J. J.   81
McKenna, William J.   52, 67
McLane, Allan   33
McLane, Robert   10, 15, 23, 28
McLaughlin, George B.   35
McNair, A. C.   89
McNemar, Oscar   77
McNue, Cla.   68
McWhirter, Edgar   76
Meade, William A.   43
Meeks, Herbert F.   71
Mehrbrei, Michael A.   71
Meisel, Frank N.   78
Melvin, Chester T.   82
Melvin, J. W. D.   89
Mencken, J. H.   86
Menshaw, Z. T.   89
Mercer, George P.   60
Merchant, Frank   68
Meredith, Alfred C.   48
Meredith, Luther H.   48
Merrick, Charles A.   41
Merrick, Wilson G.   38
Merrifield, W. R.   81
Merten, George   67
Messenger, John R.   35
Metovsky, Joseph   62
Metz, Robert W.   35
Meyer, H. F., Jr.   80
Meyer, L. W.   89
Meyers, Edward   54
Meyers, George J.   51
Michel, C. H.   89
Michel, F. G.   89
Middlekauff, H. D.   74

Middleton, James H.   48
Miller, C. W.   92
Miller, E.   53
Miller, George   71
Miller, H.   68
Miller, L. A.   56
Miller, P. Ambrose   81
Miller, Robert J.   71
Miller, Samuel   67
Miller, T.   90
Miller, Theodore   43, 90
Milley (Milnay), Jacob H.   39
Millikin, R. J.   89
Mills, A.   47
Mills, George E.   86
Mills, J. R.   83
Mills, N.   47
Milton, B. J.   86
Minnick, George R.   82
Minnick, Louis N.   82
Minton, J. L.   74
Mister, John William   64
Mitchell, George W.   50
Mitchell, Joseph B.   56
Mitchell, P. R.   46
Mitchell, Phil E.   42
Mitchell, William A.   43
Mitten, J. A.   89
Moale, John   89
Montell, Henry K.   83
Montell, Thomas J.   87
Monthly, E.   55
Moore, Alex N.   36
Moore, Arthur L.   87
Moore, August   56
Moore, Charles   54
Moore, H.   57
Moore, Herman   54
Moore, William   46
Mordecai, William C.   76
Morgan, Hugh B.   36
Morgan, James   48
Morgan, John A.   40 - 41
Morgenroth, H.   60
Morgenroth, Oscar   75
Morison, H. W.   91
Morrison, David   71
Morrison, M. L.   89
Morrison, T. E.   54
Moulden, Harry   46
Mowbray, William   37
Moyrich, R. F.   56
Mudge, George T.   80
Mullikin, H. Franklin   92

Mullin, P. 54
Munoz, E. A. 85
Murphy, C. R. 79
Murphy, William M. 80
Murrill, C. E. 54
Muth, John A. 65
Myers (Meyers), David V. 43
Myers, Charles E. 49
Myers, Louis B. 49
Myrick, Robert (Richard) F. 63

N

Nagel, Henry 81
Naylor, Lawrence A. 91
Neary, A. G. 51
Neilson, G. H. 91
Nelson, Benjamin 43
Nelson, T. T. 84
Neubert, Joseph L. 59
Newton, Henry J. 66
Newton, Howard H. 57
Newton, J. E. 76
Newton, Samuel T. 82
Nicholas, G. S. 92
Nicholas, T. J. R. 91
Nichols, Thomas D. 50
Niewerth, A. C. 79
Nininger, Charles M. 86
Niven, Edwin B. 93
Noakes, William 87
Norris, Harry 58
Norris, James F. 39
Numsen, J. Newman 91
Nusz, H. F. 76

O

O'Brien, Philip E. 63
O'Brien, R. E. 79
O'Brien, Thomas F. 63
O'Brien, William W. 76
O'Conner, Fergus 72
O'Hara, Charles 35
O'Neill, John E. 79
O'Neill, John M. 35
O'Toulan, M. F. 82
Obery, Charles H. 50
Obery, William J. 50
Obitz, Lawrence 66
Offutt, William W. 47
Ogburn, Charlie 86
Old, F. E. 77
Oler, William H. 91
Oliver, Harry M. 59
Orndorff, J. R. 84

Osbourn, John F. 80
Ouesta, J. 58
Owen, F. Buchanan 73
Owens, Albert S. J. 15
Owens, Daniel 85
Owens, H. Winter 45

P

Packard, Joseph 47
Packham, C. H. T. 89
Page, C. R. 34
Page, Charles B. 93
Page, Milton 41
Page, William E. 41
Painter, L. G. 73
Paisal, W. Vernon 65
Palmer, R. McGill 73
Pardee, John S. E. 48
Parker, Clarence 37
Parkhurst, L. B. 55
Parkinson, Joseph 43
Parks, J. Magness 57
Parks, Lawson 38
Parrish, L. E. 55
Parrott, George W. 41
Parvis, Joseph M. 24, 48
Pass, William 46
Passley, T. 52, 85
Patterson, C. R. 84
Patterson, John H. 73
Patterson, William 41
Paxon, E. H. 78
Peck, Emil 60
Pelton, James 35
Pennell, Hazen 43
Pennell, Joseph R. 49
Pennington, D. F. 50
Pentz, Stanley H. 80
Percival, James J. 74
Percy, E. 37
Peregoy, Wilbur B. 76
Perkins, Boyd W. 86
Perkins, J. A. 51
Peters, Andrew (Andy) 54
Peters, C. G. 90
Peters, Charles J. 60
Peters, J. 58
Peu...inan (illegible), E. O. 91
Pfanmuller (Pfaninueler), Henry F. 65
Pfluger, C. J. 52
Phelan, N. 55
Phillips, Charles H. 87
Phillips, Harry 78
Piehler, F. W. 74

Pines, Alex 70
Pines, William 70
Pitt, R. T. 82
Pitt, W. B. 82
Plantholt, George J. 85
Plassil, John 60
Plumley, J. R. 80
Plummer, Edward 83
Plummer, Pinkney H. 82
Poe, R. Johnson 71
Poligardo, S. 84
Polk, H. R. 91
Pomelle, Edward B. 73
Poole, W. H. 54
Pope, G. W. 89
Pope, Micajah W. 71
Porter, David D. 85
Porter, H. Morton 35
Porter, James C. 34
Porter, Phil E. 24 - 25, 42
Poss, C. J. 47
Potts, Oscar 40
Pouder (Ponder), J. M. 80
Prather, J. B., Jr. 75
Preston, Claude 35
Preston, Reynolds 39
Preston, William L. 35
Price, Arthur B. 87
Price, Harry W. 83
Price, John W. 56
Pritchard, Irvin L. 85
Purnell, Howard T. 60
Purnell, William G. 34
Putsche, Thomas F. 72
Putts, William E. 92
Pyle, William J. 64

Q
Quillen, James H. 64

R
Rabbitt, Charles 47
Rabbitt, Harvey 47
Racine, Harry 40
Radcliffe, R. W. 89
Ratcliff, P. R. 55
Rathbun, H. J. 60
Rawlins, Louis M. 71
Ray, Guy 34, 89
Rayne, J. E. 52
Read, F. T. 80
Reading, W. M. 46
Reckord, Milton A. 38
Redner, Herman C. 59
Reeb (Reib), John 67
Reed, J. 55
Reed, J. B. T. 74
Reeder, Clinton 40
Reeder, Harvey 40
Reese, George 58
Reese, Howard 37
Reeside, John E. 93
Reeves, A. J. 62
Reilly, Charles E. 79
Reilly, J. P. 61
Reinecke, William H. 69
Reiner, Jacob 54
Reinfelder, Joseph J. 65
Renehan, W. 51
Rever, Frederick 63
Reynolds, Clarence 34
Reynolds, Clarence S. 73
Reynolds, Frank M. 39
Reynolds, George 54
Reynolds, Lloyd William 84
Rice, L. 57
Rice, L. G. 51
Richardson, J. Newman 33
Richardson, John V. 11, 59
Richardson, R. W. 89
Ricketts, C. 46
Ricketts, Preston 47
Ricketts, R. J. 47
Rider, John 67
Ridgely, Charles R. 89
Ridgely, G. W. 75
Ridgely, Gustave W. 26
Riggs, Clinton L. 17
Riggs, Douglass 47
Riggs, Laurie H. 73
Riggs, Lawrason 2 - 3, 5, 7 - 8, 12, 14 - 17, 19, 23, 26 - 28, 33
Riggs, Samuel of R. 34
Riley, Herbert 64
Riley, Hugh R. 28, 49
Riley, John E. 56
Rine, G. D. 54
Ripplemeyer, Leo 67
Ritchey, William M. 35
Rittenhouse, D. M. 53
Rittenhouse, J. E. 4, 24, 65
Ritter, John M. 79
Ritter, Leopold J. 77
Rivialles, F. T. 52
Robbins, Ed, Jr. 72
Roberts, C. H. 52
Roberts, Charles S. 45
Roberts, James L. 48

Robertson, H. E. 64
Robinson, C. H. 78
Robinson, George T. 50
Robinson, William 52
Rockel, August 69
Rockel, George 69
Roe, J. Wesley 48
Roeder, J. A. 55
Rogers, A. P. 80
Rogers, C. Lyon, Jr. 91
Rogers, James L. 91
Rogers, Thornton 88
Rohleder, Thomas J. 62
Rooney, William 67
Roosevelt, Theodore 17 - 18, 20, 27 - 28
Rose, Lewis 69
Rose, William F. 63
Rosenstock, G. E. 52
Rosenthal (Rozenthal), William B. 69
Roseway, Adam J. 55
Rosner, Sterling D. 38
Ross, Frank 69
Ross, Frank B. 86
Ross, Joseph W. 40
Rothwell, Edward K. 48
Rourke, Frank 60
Rouston, William A. 38
Rowe, Moumonier 25 - 26, 60
Rowe, Robert B. 36
Ruark, S. L. 46
Ruby, Charles F. 57
Rulhnan (Rullman), William 50
Rupp, Frederick W. 65
Rupp, Walter S. 86
Ruppert, Frank 35
Rusk, Harry Welles, Jr. 83
Russell, Charles I. 83
Russell, Edward H. 76
Rusteberg, Charles A. 87
Rutter, George W. 40
Ryley, J. Frank 25, 51

S

Sachs, (Abe?) 68
Sader, John I. 84
Samsell, John M. 76
Sands, Frank N. 91
Sands, Thomas E. 42
Sands, William E. 36
Sauks (Sanks), E. L. 58
Saxton, Oscar 66
Sayler, J. A. 50
Schaeffer, Charles F., Jr. 57
Schafer (Schaefer), John C. 60
Scharf, C. E. 90
Schiere, Joseph L. 59
Schiminger, John C. 69
Schine (Shire), Joseph L. 59
Schleuther, Herman 63
Schley, Harry J. 35
Schmidt, C. E. 82
Schmidt, John H. 68
Schmidt, William 65
Schnebelen, Edward 66
Schnur, B. A. 82
Scholpp, Charles 39
Schuchart, John J. 83
Schultz, Charles H. 76
Schwartz, William 71
Scott, Frank 41
Scott, J. W. 74
Scott, John C. 78
Scott, R. 68
Scott, Robert J. 69
Sears, Cheston B. 49
Sears, George W. 49
Sears, Samuel J. 49
Sebald, Philipp 63
Seward, Edward 70
Sewell, Joseph C. 62
Seymore, J. B. 77
Shaffer, Luther Porter 74
Shane, John H. 87
Shanks, Walter L. 58
Shannon, John T. 82
Sharar, Walter 36
Shelley, H. 58
Shelton, C. M. 80
Shelton, Ross T. 62
Shenley (Shancley), James 52
Shepherd, F. B. 73
Shepherd, Percy M. 82
Sheridan, J. Robert 76
Sherman, A. K. 63
Shertzer, Harry A. 39
Shields, William C. 53
Shipe, Charles A. 35
Shipley, Arthur H. 72
Shipley, C. R. 54
Shipley, Charles F. 79
Shipley, Edward A. 63
Shipley, Harry 70
Shipley, J. H. 78
Shirley, H. C., Jr. 91
Shirley, John D. 36
Shirley, Joseph W. 33, 91
Shoppelman (Coppelman), John 61

Shorey, M. C. 80
Shriver, Edward S. 44
Sieling, H. J. W. 91
Simmon, John 68
Simmons, F. R. 82
Simmons, Frank H. 55
Simon, J. 55
Simon, John 62
Simonson, H. A. 45
Simpers, Edgar T. 41
Sindall, Robert A. 81
Sindell, J. H. 84
Singer, Max 37
Sipes, D. L. 78
Slate, E. M. 89
Slingluff, (W.) 72
Slingluff, D. H. 73
Slingluff, Horace, Jr. 72
Slingluff, Jesse 12, 26, 86
Slonaker, Harry B. 56
Slone, Henry 68
Small, Joseph T. 50
Small, Ruben K. 36
Smith, A. H. 75
Smith, Arthur 69
Smith, Arthur J. 42
Smith, C. W. 46
Smith, Charles A. 82
Smith, Charles H. 66
Smith, Charles W. 56
Smith, Claude Tilden 43
Smith, Cleveland S. 41
Smith, E. A. 75
Smith, Ed. F. 53
Smith, George 53
Smith, George W. 50
Smith, Harry L. 62
Smith, Herbert A. 88
Smith, L. 70
Smith, Louis A. 35
Smith, R. E., Jr. 90
Smith, Randolph R. 77
Smith, Roy E. 46
Smith, Sidney 63
Smith, Silas B. 38
Smith, Stuart 34
Smith, Wilbur C. 79
Smith, William A. 80
Smith, William H. 82
Smithson, Ivan 76
Sneed, Harry B. 56
Snooks, Harry E. 62
Snyder, Harry E. 77
Snyder, William W. 78

Soulsby, C. M. T. 41
Spamer, J. A. 77
Sparklin(g), Fredrick 42
Sparks, George W. 79
Sparks, William S. 48
Spence, C. R. 33
Spencer, Cecil C. 38
Sponheimer, Henry 87
Sprecher, Emory R. 36
Spruill, St. Clair 71
Stahlkneckt (Stallkneckt), Edward 62
Staisloff, Charles 66
Stapf, George W. 63
Starkloff, C. V. 33
Starr, Asel 39
Staubs, Jesse L. 57
Staubs, Robert C. 66
Staylor, John S. 60
Steiner, W. L. 55
Sterling, Frank P. 41
Stern, T. F. 91
Sterner, H. J. 86
Stesch, Ed. H. J. 68
Stevenson, James T. 78
Stevenson, John J. 77
Stevenson, William 78
Stewart, Charles 87
Stewart, J. T., Jr. 84
Stewart, Joseph T. 90
Stewart, L. H. 74
Stewart, L. R. 64
Stimpson, H. B. 91
Stone, William J. 44
Stonesifer, Edward 70
Stonesifer, Edward A. 78
Streett, Alex D. 39
Streett, E. O. 19, 28, 75
Strohm, John C. 49
Strohm, Thomas A., Jr. 83
Stump, E. A. 76
Stump, J. S., Jr. 73
Stump, Norman 91
Sturgis, H. W. 46
Summerbell, Ferris 52
Summers, Clarence A. 41
Sunderland, B. B. 92
Supplee, J. Frank 3 - 4, 23 - 24, 51
Suter, Clifton 62
Svine, Carl A. 83
Swain, Charles P. 53
Swain, James E. 56
Swain, R. C. 52
Sweeny, H. Wilson 90
Sweet, Charles A. 42

Sweeting, George 84
Swithenbank, H. L. 84
Sylvester, William W. 70

T

Taft, William Howard 17
Talbot, Thomas M. 46
Talbott, D. Russell 92
Tall, Lewis C. 36
Tarbutton, Charles M. 42
Tarbutton, Olin 42
Tavenner, M. (Michael) K. 70
Taylor, Charles N. 50
Taylor, E. M. 80
Taylor, E. R. 82
Taylor, Frank B. 50
Taylor, G. W. 53
Taylor, James, Jr. 83
Taylor, John N. 49
Taylor, W. R. 51
Teano, S. 84
Tegeler (Tegelir), Albert 70
Templeman, F. Leroy 73
Thomas, Clark 51
Thomas, Douglas 78
Thomas, J. E. 53
Thomas, J. Edward 53
Thomas, James 81
Thomas, T. R. 78
Thomas, William E. 50
Thompson, A. B. 80
Thompson, Arthur 86
Thompson, B. M. 74
Thompson, Charles 43
Thompson, E. 68
Thompson, George A. 41
Thompson, H. F. 76
Thompson, W. C. 90
Thomson, Elbert 75
Thomson, James H. 44
Times, Alex 53
Tinsley, Frank 81
Tinson, Clarence 53
Tompkins, John A. 93
Tonry, Albert S. 85
Topscott, W. 90
Townsend, Charles T. 88
Townsend, W. Guy 25, 51
Towson, W. E. 82
Tracey, E. C. 58
Tracey, R. J. 80
Trago, Harris 39
Trail, Carlton 47
Trammell, Joseph E. 47

Treffinger, H. H. 65
Tregellas, S. Staley 91
Trescott, Joseph 58
Trice, V. Calvin 37
Trimble, Walter 67
Tripp, E. R. 34
Trogood, Charles 52
Trone, Franklin A. 36
Trott, S. W. 60
Truitt, J. H. 75
Truman, W. E. 78
Tschautre (Tschantre), Leon E. 37
Tucker, Laurence 38
Tucker, N. C. 37
Tull, James 43
Turner, Benjamin W. 45
Turner, George J. 72, 82
Turner, Henry P. 41
Turner, John P. 89
Turner, Ray 48
Turner, William F. 63
Tydings, George R. 24, 42
Tydings, George T. 42
Tyler, Douglas 52
Tynenson (Tynerson), Arthur A. 36

U

Uhler (Uhlen), W. D. 50
Ullrich, Harry 35
Ullrich, S. S. 50
Undutch, John 61
Undutch, Joseph 11
Upshur, George M. 2 - 3, 26
Upton, John 67

V

Van Fassen, Dudley H. 44
Van Fassen, Irvin J. 44
Van Stavonen, James E. 70
Vane, Roy C. (Leroy) 37
Vanous, William J. 49
Vansant, Hiram D. 89
Varian, H. L. 78
Vasey, Horace 48
Vesper, John 40
Vessel, George H. 57
Vicari, S. 84
Vogel, Henry 65
Vogeler, Fred 70
Vogler, Herman E., Jr. 87
Volanfer (Volaufer), George W. 67
Vollman, Walter 60
Von Hagel, Charles 67

Von Hagel, William 67
Voneiff, Craft W. 68

W

Wachter (Wachner), Edward J. 64
Wagner, Fred H. 92
Wagner, Harry 87
Wagner, William C. 61
Wain, Charles W. 65
Wain, Howard 66
Walker, Joe 69
Walker, Percy L. 87
Wallace, Allen 37
Wallace, Robert B. 42
Waller, William 37
Walling, Harry 58
Walstrom, William 61
Walter, William M. 79
Walterhofer, Charles G. (S.) 64
Walters, Morris 51
Wands, H. B. 78
Wanner, Arthur H. 64
Ward, Hamlet 76
Ward, William H. 49
Ward, William R. 87
Warfield, Edwin 12, 14, 16 - 17, 26 - 28
Warfield, Henry M. 3, 5 - 6, 23 - 24
Warfield, Henry Mactier 71
Warfield, Leroy C. 59
Warkmeister, Louis 57
Warner, W. 69
Warnick, John 39
Warren, Herbert H. 48
Warrington, William E. 42
Waters, Clark 47
Waters, H. Burton 39
Watkins, Burton 39
Watson, D. B. 75
Watson, James O. 39
Watson, L. H. 56
Watts, C. R. 51
Wayne, James 67
Webb, W. D. 84
Weber, Abram 75
Weber, Harvey E. (C.) 35
Weber, Mervin 65
Webster, C. T. 86
Webster, Elisha B. 44
Webster, Horace 62
Weeks, William W. 44
Weems, F. S. 54
Wehrenberg, Fred 66
Weidenheimer, George 66

Weigh, John N. 43
Weilbenner, Louis 67
Weise, Edward 54
Weissenborn, Fred M. 56
Wells, Henry S. 89
Wentworth, S. T. 77
Wessels, A. L., MD. 57
Wessels, Asa L. 23
West, Joe 47
Weston, Harry J. 42
Wheeler, Charles H. 64
Wherrett, Harry 37
Whipp, Arthur 47
White, Andrew J. C. 65
White, Charles H. 79
White, James C. (Clinton) 78
White, James G. 35
White, John L. 69
White, N. W. 55
White, W. W. 46
Whiteford, Frank 39
Whitman, F. S. 83
Whitman, Walter W. 41
Whitney, W. 78
Whitney, Wilber B. 81
Whitty, William 82
Wickham, William H. 83
Wiesenborn, F. 58
Wiggin, D. C. 52
Wiggins, T. B. 52
Wildason, John 39
Wilkinson, F. 58
Wilkinson, Pinkney W. 93
Willard, Edwin G. 92
Willey, Frank 38
Williams, A. (Addine) 53
Williams, Benjamin C. 70
Williams, C. H. 57
Williams, Edward 70
Willis, E. S. 55
Wilmer, J. C. 74
Wilson 93
Wilson, Charles H. 63
Wilson, Edward 37
Wilson, Ephraim B. 89
Wilson, Harry T. 87
Wilson, John E. 48
Wilson, Louis S. 91
Wilson, W. B. 85
Windle, Ed 60
Windle, John M. 57
Winslow, N. 55
Winterson, John C. P. 88
Wirth, G. G., Jr. 75

Wirz, Ernest 37
Wischmeyer, Ed, Jr. 51
Wisotzki, G. C. 90
Witzgall, Walter 69
Wolf, Edward 63
Wolfe, J. W. 82
Wood, Ernest P. 49
Wood, J. H. 34
Wood, Walter B. 41
Wooden, H. E. 51
Wooden, James H. 65
Wooden, S. 53
Wooden, William T. 52
Woodey, John F. 75
Woodruff, Charles T. 93
Woods, Harry E. 61
Woodside, E. L. 33
Woolford, Henry C. 48
Workmeister, Louis 71
Worley, A. 84
Worstman, Frank 70
Wright, Edwin O. 78
Wright, George 40
Wright, Lyle 37
Wright, Walter C. 56
Wright, William A. 34
Wright, William T. 40
Wroth, John 93
Wyatt, E. L. 82
Wyman, S. J. 82
Wynn, Harry L. 72

Y

Yard, Harold 72
Yewell, Walter H. 42
Young, (Joe?) 68
Young, Benjamin G. 65
Young, Cyrus C. 87
Young, Edgar K. 88
Young, J. Forney 91
Younger, Thomas J. 77

Z

Zeller, Joseph 65
Zendgraft, Joseph F. (T.) 44
Zendgraft, William D. 45
Zentgraf, Joseph F. 55
Zimmermann, George H. 61
Zinkand, John S. 36
Zipprian, Edward 59
Zollinhofer, William 63

www.ingramcontent.com/pod-product-compliance
Lightning Source LLC
Chambersburg PA
CBHW070504100426
42743CB00010B/1754